Glovebox
Guides

Galveston

TEXAS 1998

PUBLISHER'S NOTE:

The making of maps is, for the most part, a matter of reconciling spherical and planar geometry .... the entirely pragmatic need to depict a three-dimensional surface on a sheet of paper. The nature of the problem is intractable for it is quite incapable of accomplishment and without exception every method ever devised has an inherent disadvantage when put to practical use.

This work is drawn according to Mercator's Projection and is based on the United States Department of Commerce map 'Galveston and Texas City Harbors', Sheet 11324. It conforms, in general, to the North American Datum of 1983 which is taken to be equivalent to the World Geodetic System of 1984.

Mercator was born of German parents in 1512 and became the foremost cartographer of his age. In his day latitude could be estimated with reasonable accuracy but the estimation of longitude presented acute problems in stellar observation and calculation. Therefore, the system of horizontal lines of latitude and vertical lines of longitude, which we take for granted, although understood by a few cartographers was rarely, if ever, used for practical navigational purposes.

Mercator was well aware of the practicalities of navigating a ship and set himself the task of devising a map whereby a straight connecting line between two points would give a constant compass bearing. On such a map a mariner could draw a line to define ANY course secure in the knowledge that if he sailed his ship at the required heading he would make his landfall without the constant imperative to estimate latitude and distance run.

THE GUIDE

He eventually devised a method, which he published in 1569, based on the premise that the spherical earth be enclosed by a true cylinder that only touches the earth along its equator. His insight was to project known points on the globe outwards until they intersected the enclosing cylinder. When the cylinder is unwrapped, point-to-point compass bearings are depicted as straight lines on a rectilinear grid aligned with the earth's equator.

This apparent navigational simplicity is achieved at the cost of grossly distorting land masses at high latitudes, the 'Greenland Effect'. In practice, as so few people live above the 60th. North parallel and even fewer below the 60th. South, this constraint has had little practical importance and more modern maps employ his system than any other.

This matter is mentioned here because the following maps show the relevant lines of longitude and latitude for GPS (Global Positioning System) purposes. In Mercator's system vertical distortion is proportional to the reciprocal of the sine of latitude and in this context Galveston is uniquely placed. The Island lies slightly below the 29th. parallel at an angle of about 40 degrees North by East. At this latitude it happens that one DEGREE of longitude is defined by approximately 60.055 miles, from which it follows one MINUTE of longitude is VERY slightly more than a mile and the corresponding minute of latitude is about 1.14 miles. Thus, the linear scales given here only really apply to the East/West axis.

Obviously, all this appears to be somewhat esoteric but the Publisher's objective is to eventually correct the computer database from which these maps are derived such that all the delineated features will be within the present commercial GPS margin of error (about 15yards). In its present form the work is not as accurate as this but the Publisher is reasonably confident it will put a GPS user well within sight of the indicated position over the entire road system of the Island.

THE GUIDE continued

ORGANIZATION.

TIKI & PELICAN ISLANDS

SCHOLES FIELD - A summary of relevant aviation information

THE CITY - Mapped at 6 inches to the mile as far as Anderson Ways

THE WESTERN COMMUNITIES Mapped at 4 inches to the mile

Each page overlaps its neighbors on all four sides and each page has six location squares;   A, B, C, D, E, & F.

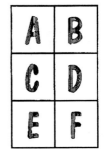

The Street Lists give Page Numbers and Location squares.

ADVERTISING:

Glovebox Guides, Route 1, Box 1646 DICKINSON, TX 77539

THE GUIDE

DISCLAIMER:

The publisher believed the Guide to be substantially accurate at the time of publication and it is offered for sale on the clear understanding that GLOVEBOX GUIDES is not to be held responsible for ANY form of inconvenience, damage, or loss to either life, or property, arising from its use.

COPYRIGHT

This publication is protected by U.S. Copyright Law. It is illegal to reproduce it in any form, by any means, either in whole or in part, without the formal consent of GLOVEBOX GUIDES. However, bona-fide users are free to use THE GUIDE TO GALVESTON in any way they wish for their OWN, AND LIMITED, PRIVATE PURPOSES..

ACKNOWLEDGMENTS:

Mr. Greg Thomas, Glovebox Guides' computer consultant ......whose expertise made the GUIDE possible. "I don't care how fast the machines run now - make them run faster...and faster.......and faster!"

The aerial photographs, on which most of the topographic detail is based, were taken from Cessna 150's piloted by Carl Bentley of Galv-Aero Flight Center and Shawn Olanyk of Golden Eagle Aviation.

Niva Wilkinson compiled the 'WordPerfect' street indexes.

Ron R. Surovik of the Port of Galveston provided the basis for the dock information shown here.

Shelly Kelly of the Rosenberg Library provided most of the information concerning Tiki Island.

Joan Hoffman and Barbara Wertz, of the now defunct Galveston Economic Development Corporation.

Marsha Wilson ......who has looked after Distribution.

The Ordinary People of Galveston who answered my dammed-fool questions with great patience and allowed me to go wherever I wished.

And finally, Wanda Sue for her unstinted moral support, dubiously assisted by our friends Lizzie Loring and Smudge.

Rob Lucas-Dean   November, 1997

THE GUIDE

continued

TIKI ISLAND: BACKGROUND

Until the early 1960's Tiki Island was no more than two or three hundred acres of salt marsh to the west of the Galveston causeway. This ill-defined area terminated in the extreme west at Wilson's Point, but who Wilson was now appears to be totally forgotten! In the mid-60's the entire area was acquired by the Jamaica Corporation of Houston from the City of Galveston and in late 1965 work commenced on the construction of a 10 acre, $1.5 million marina, designed for Jamaica Corp. by Sam Shelsky, a marine architect of Fort Lauderdale, Florida, at the request of its then vice-president, Ellis Allen.   Jamaica Corp. considered this project to be sufficiently important to form a subsidiary called the Tiki Marina Company with Allen as its President.   Allen had been involved in the development of Jamaica Beach on Galveston Island and to promote the new development he adopted the easygoing Polynesian/Maori theme which dominates the island to the present day.

At this time the 'south-going' I45 bridge had been recently completed (1961) and Allen, as Houston's former Utilities Director, Real Estate Director, and finally City Treasurer, probably used his influence to extend Tiki Drive, the access road to the Marina, a mile and a half to the west in order to make Wilson's Point accessible. Consolidation of the island then began in earnest under the direction of the Timewealth Corporation in association with Noble Homes. As a result Tiki Island now covers 400 acres and comprises about 600 prime bulkheaded waterfront homes, or sites, all having deep-water access to the Intercoastal Waterway and the Gulf of Mexico.   The name 'TIKI' is central to the colorful, and extremely complex, mythology of the Maoris of New Zealand ..... and what follows is no more than a crude summary.

In the beginning the God Tane brought three baskets of Knowledge to our world. He then created the first woman by molding her in red sand, bringing her to life by means of his own breath.   Her name was Hine and by her agency Tane fathered the first man. The first woman had two aspects, or faces, in the first she symbolized 'Life', and in the second she was Guardian of the Dead. Hine also produced a daughter for Tane,

TIKI ISLAND

Hineteiwaiwa. Hineteiwaiwa became the Goddess of Childbirth and was seduced by Tane, unaware he was her father. To atone for this unnatural act she conveys Maori dead to the underworld. Tike and Hine had many other children who in turn had many liaisons with both Gods and mortals and these beings produced most of the Demi-Gods and Heros of Maori tradition.

The 'Hei-Tiki' or First Man charm shown here is characteristically made of jade. Worn as a pendant, its grotesque appearance is intended to ward off evil spirits and thus protect its wearer from bodily harm.

VIRGINIA POINT

Galveston's association with 'King Cotton' and slavery, began in the 1840's, both activities, so far as the City was concerned, being entirely concerned with exporting the raw material by sea. This situation lasted until the commencement of the Civil War by which time at least three independent railroad companies had established railheads at Virginia Point on the mainland. Each of these companies was primarily concerned with the transport of State-grown cotton and imported goods and was obliged to share access to the Port of Galveston over a single-track trestle bridge built in 1859. The strategic position of the railroads therefore obliged Federal troops to occupy Virginia Point during the Civil War, as a part of the Federal blockade of the South, and this occupation was to mark a fundamental change in Galveston's fortunes.

While the Union held the bridge, the Confederacy supplied the City from the sea and held it until it surrendered on June 19, 1865. Although Galveston, and Cotton, prospered under 'Reconstruction', following the Civil War, and again after the turmoil of the first World War, its period of isolation under the 'stars and bars' forced the development of alternative access to the sea and initiated the economic supremacy of Houston. .....

Today virtually nothing remains of the 19th. century railhead at Virginia Point

TIKI ISLAND BACKGROUND
continued

A

Admiral Circle	Tb A

B

Bamaku Bend	Tb C
Bamboo	Ta F, Tb E
Bora Bora	Tb D, F

C

Castaway	Ta F
Catamaran	Ta D
Coconut	Ta D
Commander	Ta C
Copra	Ta F
Coral Way	Tb C

D

Diamond Drive	Ta D

E

Easterly Drive	Ta C

H

Harbour Circle	Ta C
Hawaii	Tb E
Head Road	Ta D

I

Isles East Road	Ta C

K

Kam Me Ha	Ta D

L

Leilani Drive	Tb C
Lokai	Tb D
Lotus	Ta F

M

Mango Drive	Tb C
Matatea	Tb C
Maui	Tb E
Moorea	Tb D

O

Oahu	Tb D
Outrigger Drive	Tb D

P

Palmetto	Ta E
Papeete	Tb D
Paradise Drive	Tb D
Port O'Call	Ta C, E

Q

Quayside	Tb D, F

S

Short Reach	Tb D

T

Tahiti	Tb C
Tamana	Tb C, E
Tiki Circle	Tc C
Tiki Drive	Ta C, Tb D, Tc C

W

Wahini	Tb C
Windward Way	Tb D

TIKE ISLAND CITY HALL	802 Tiki Drive	TX77554		(409) 935 1427
Emergency			911	
Mayor's Office				(409) 935 9199
Marshall's Office				(409) 935 6579
Volunteer Fire Department				(409) 935 6579
Galveston County Fresh Water				(409) 935 1486
Supply Department No. 6				
Tiki Island Civic Association	802 Tiki Drive	TX 77551		(409) 938 0120
TIKE ISLAND INFORMATION CENTER				
THE PRUDENTIAL - Tiki Realty Co.	100 Tiki Drive	TX 77551		(409) 938 4807
Tiki Island Store	200 Tiki Drive	TX 77554		(409) 935 1782
Teakwood Marina & Restaurant	400 Tiki Drive	TX 77554		(409) 935 5552
Nita Bell Realtors	400 Tiki Drive	TX 77551		(409) 935 7723

TIKI ISLAND

Street Location

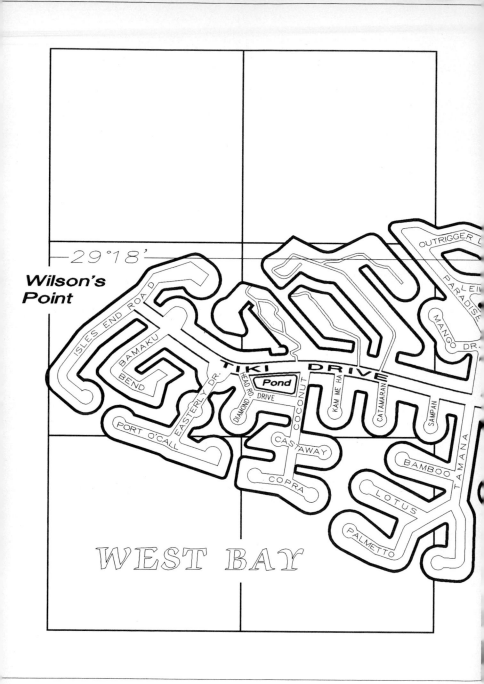

29°18′

Wilson's Point

ISLES END ROAD

BAMAKU BEND

PORT O'CALL

EASTERLY DR.

TIKI DRIVE

HEAD RD. DRIVE

Pond

DIAMOND

CASTAWAY

COCONUT

COPRA

KAM ME HA

CATAMARAN

SAMPAN

BAMBOO

TAMANA

LOTUS

PALMETTO

OUTRIGGER L

PARADISE LEIW

MANGO DR.

WEST BAY

Ta TIKI ISLAND:

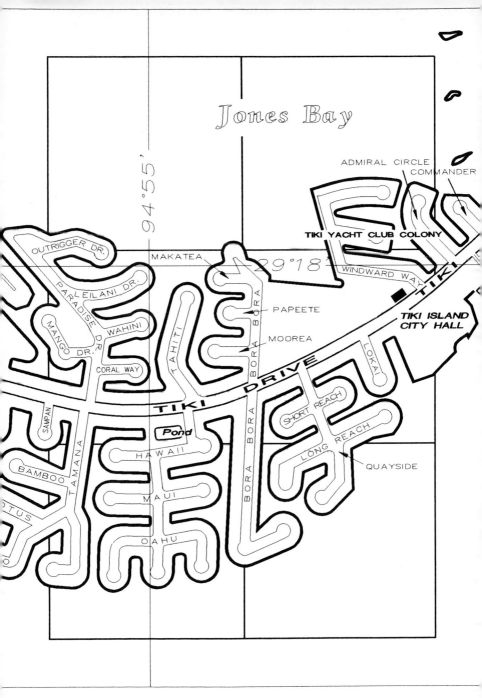

Jones Bay

94°55'

ADMIRAL CIRCLE
COMMANDER

TIKI YACHT CLUB COLONY

MAKATEA

29°18'

WINDWARD WAY

TIKI

OUTRIGGER DR.

PARADISE DR.
LEILANI DR.

MANGO DR.
WAHINI

CORAL WAY

TAHITI

BORA BORA

PAPEETE

MOOREA

TIKI ISLAND
CITY HALL

LOKAI

TIKI DRIVE

SAMPAN

Pond

HAWAII

BORA BORA

SHORT REACH

LONG REACH

QUAYSIDE

BAMBOO

TAMANA

MAUI

LOTUS

OAHU

Area: Approx.
400 acres

1/3 MILE
SQUARES

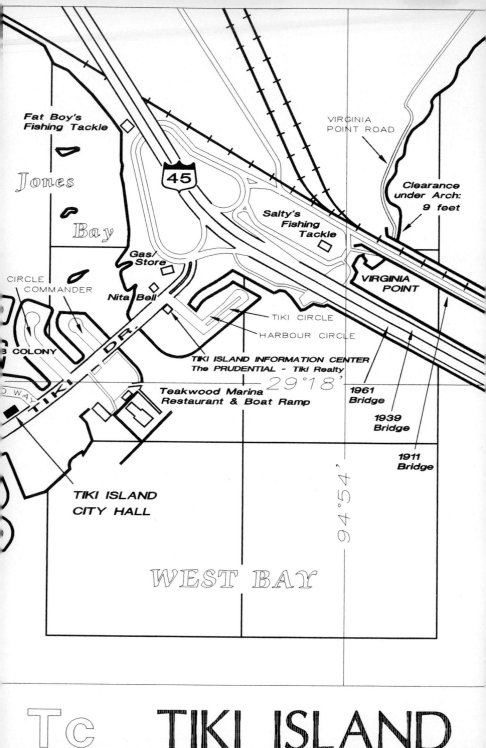

Fat Boy's
Fishing Tackle

Jones

Bay

45

VIRGINIA
POINT ROAD

Salty's
Fishing
Tackle

Clearance
under Arch:
9 feet

CIRCLE
COMMANDER

Gas/
Store

VIRGINIA
POINT

Nita Bell

B COLONY

TIKI CIRCLE

HARBOUR CIRCLE

TIKI ISLAND INFORMATION CENTER
The PRUDENTIAL - Tiki Realty

29°18'

1961
Bridge

Teakwood Marina
Restaurant & Boat Ramp

1939
Bridge

1911
Bridge

TIKI ISLAND
CITY HALL

94°54'

WEST BAY

Tc   TIKI ISLAND

The Stewart Title Company Building
222 Kempner Street

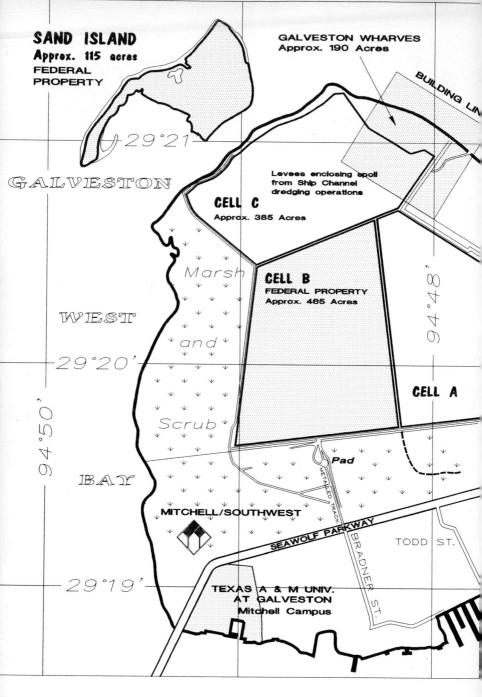

SAND ISLAND
Approx. 115 acres
FEDERAL
PROPERTY

GALVESTON WHARVES
Approx. 190 Acres

BUILDING LIN

29°21'

GALVESTON

Levees enclosing spoil
from Ship Channel
dredging operations

CELL C
Approx. 385 Acres

CELL B
FEDERAL PROPERTY
Approx. 465 Acres

94°48'

WEST

Marsh

29°20'

and

94°50'

Scrub

CELL A

BAY

Pad

METALLED TRACK

MITCHELL/SOUTHWEST

SEAWOLF PARKWAY

BRADNER ST.

TODD ST.

29°19'

TEXAS A & M UNIV.
AT GALVESTON
Mitchell Campus

PELICAN ISLAND

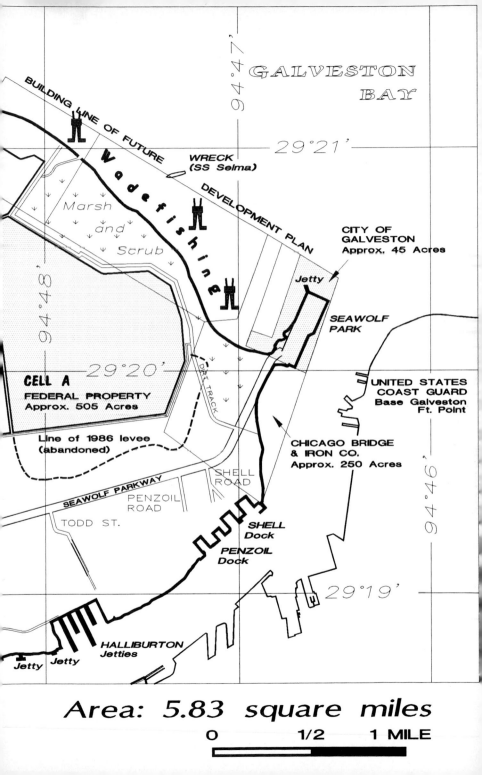

GALVESTON BAY

94°47'

29°21'

BUILDING LINE OF FUTURE

DEVELOPMENT PLAN

WRECK
(SS Selma)

Wadefishing

Marsh
and
Scrub

94°48'

CITY OF
GALVESTON
Approx. 45 Acres

Jetty

SEAWOLF
PARK

29°20'

DIRT TRACK

CELL A
FEDERAL PROPERTY
Approx. 505 Acres

UNITED STATES
COAST GUARD
Base Galveston
Ft. Point

Line of 1986 levee
(abandoned)

CHICAGO BRIDGE
& IRON CO.
Approx. 250 Acres

SEAWOLF PARKWAY

PENZOIL
ROAD

SHELL
ROAD

94°46'

TODD ST.

SHELL
Dock

PENZOIL
Dock

29°19'

HALLIBURTON
Jetties

Jetty   Jetty

Area: 5.83 square miles

0   1/2   1 MILE

AIRPORT IDENTIFICATION & FACILITIES

SCHOLES FLD (GLS)   3SW   UTC-C(-5DT)

N29°16' W49°52'   HOUSTON   7   B   S4

Fuel   100   JET A
Traffic Pattern Altitude: 1000 F/W - 500 HELI
Airport Of Entry: One hour's notice required
Certified Airport (FAR 139):   ARFF Index A

RWY 17-35:   S-30   D-45   DT-90   MIRL
RWY 17:   REIL   PAPI (P4L)-GA30°TCH49'
RWY 35:   REIL   PAPI (P4L)-GA30°TCH49' Pole
RWY 13-31:   S-30   D-45   DT-90   HIRL
RWY 13: MALSR PAPI (P4L)-GA30°TCH49' Crane
RWY 31:   REIL   PAPI (P4L)-GA30°TCH49' Pole

OPERATING HOURS: 08.00 TO 22.00
CLOSED TO 30-SEAT COMMERCIAL AIRCRAFT

Flight Notification Service Available - ADCUS
Emergency Fuel Service   -   Tel. (409) 740 ????
FBO - Gulf Coast Jet Center - Tel. (409) 740 4359
RUNWAY 13 MALSR ACTIVATION: 13-CTAF

BEWARE OF HELICOPTERS

COMMUNICATIONS: CTAF/UNICOM 123.05
Montgom. Cnty FSS: (CXO)TF   1-800-WX-BRIEF
(CXO) FSS 122.2 & 122.15   and   NOTAM FILE GLS

NAVIGATION AIDS: CTAF/UNICOM 123.05
(L)VORTACW 113.0   VUH   Chan.77
ILS 111.7   I-GLS   Unmonitored

CITY OF GALVESTON MUNICIPAL AIRPORT

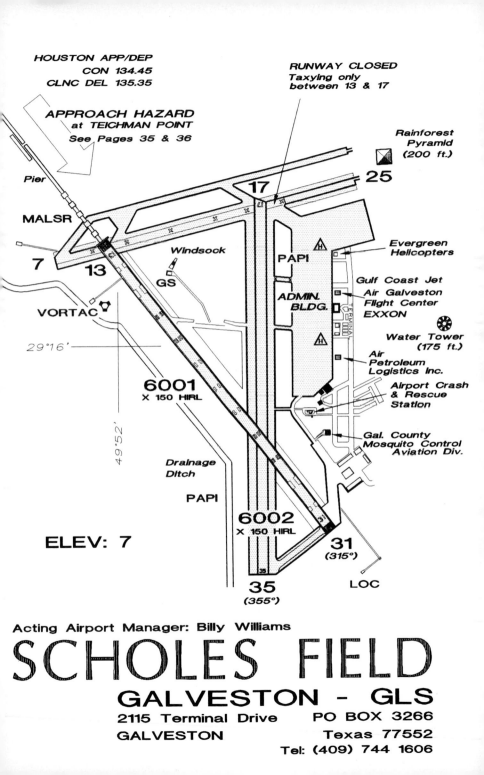

HOUSTON APP/DEP
CON 134.45
CLNC DEL 135.35

RUNWAY CLOSED
Taxiing only
between 13 & 17

APPROACH HAZARD
at TEICHMAN POINT
See Pages 35 & 36

Rainforest
Pyramid
(200 ft.)

Pier

25

MALSR

17

7

13

Windsock

PAPI

Evergreen
Helicopters

GS

ADMIN.
BLDG.

Gulf Coast Jet
Air Galveston
Flight Center
EXXON

VORTAC

Water Tower
(175 ft.)

29°16'

Air
Petroleum
Logistics Inc.

6001
X 150 HIRL

Airport Crash
& Rescue
Station

49°52'

Gal. County
Mosquito Control
Aviation Div.

Drainage
Ditch

PAPI

6002
X 150 HIRL

ELEV: 7

31
(315°)

LOC

35
(355°)

Acting Airport Manager: Billy Williams

SCHOLES FIELD

GALVESTON - GLS

2115 Terminal Drive   PO BOX 3266
GALVESTON   Texas 77552
Tel: (409) 744 1606

A

THE CITY

Street	Location
Barracuda Ave.	12C
Baudeliare Cir.	47B
Bay Meadows	35E,44B
Bayou Front Ln.	38B
Bayou Circle Dr.	28D
Bayou Homes Dr.	39A
Bayou Shore Dr.	28D
Bayside Ave.	25B,26A
Beacon	46B
Beard Drive	49E
Beech	37F
Belo	29C
Beluche Dr.	38F,47B
	48A
Bernardo De Galvez Ave.	29E,30C
(Ave. P)	31B,32A
	33D,38B
Bernice Drive	49E
Bertolino's View	22B
(10th. St.)	
Biovu Drive	39A
Bluebonnet Ct	39C
Blume St.	25C,46F
(89th)	51B
Bob Smith Rd.	60A,61A
Boddeker Drive	4A,5C
(South Jetty Rd)	
Bonanza	46B
Bonita Ave.	12C
Borden Ave.	28D,29C
Bowie Drive	29D
Brandner St.	9A
Broadway St.	19E,20E
Broadway St.	21C,29A
Broome Rd.	44D,45E
Bryan	35F

C

Street	Location
Cadena Dr.	45E
Caduceus Place	41A
Campbell Lane	28D
Campeche Cir.	45E
Campeche Cove	45E
Campeche Cove Blvd.	50A
Campeche Dr.	45E
Campeche E St.	45F
Cedar Lawn Dr. S	30B
Cedar Lawn Cir.	29B,30A
Cedar Lawn Dr. N	30A
Central City Blvd.	39F
Channe View Dr.	25B,26A
Chantilly Cir.	47D

Street	Location
Chataignon Pl	22A
(13th. St.)	
Cherokee	37F,38E
Christopher Columbus	11E,22A
Church St.	12E,18E
(Ave F)	19D,20C
	21B,22A
	23A
Cloud Lane	44B,45A
Colony Park Cir.	39E
Colony Park Dr.	39E
Copilot Lane	35F
Cosy Cove	24F
Crockett Blvd.	40B,41A
Cypress Drive	39C

D

Street	Location
Dansby Drive	39E
Darcy Drive	35C
Darrell Royal Blvd.	11F,12E
Dolphin Ave.	12C
Dominique Dr.	46D,47A
Driftwood Lane	39A

E

Street	Location
East Beach Dr.	4F,12F
East Beach Dr.	13D,14A
El Cielo	48A
Elm St.	38F

F

Street	Location
Fairway Dr.	39C
Fannin Dr.	29D
Ferry St.	2E,12A
(2nd. St.)	
Fort Point Rd.	2C,12A
Fort Crockett Blvd.	40D,41C
Frazier Ave.	28D,29E
Front Lane	38B

G

Street	Location
Garfield Dr.	49E
Gerol Cir.	38F
Gerol Court	38F
Gerol Dr.	38F
Grover Ave.	39B
Gulf Lane	12C
Gulfcrest Dr.	39F
Gull Dr.	40D

Street Location

THE CITY

P

Palm Cir.	40A
Park St.	39C
Park Lane	39E
Pearl Lane	2E
Pelican Island Causeway	7D,18A
Penzoil Rd.	10B
Pine St.	38F,48A
(74th St.)	
Pilot Lane	35D
Piper	37F
Pompano Ave.	12A
Poplar Dr.	38F,39E
Post Office St.	12E,18E
(Ave. E)	21B,22A
Princeton St.	47E
Preston	35E
Pruitt Dr.	25B,26A

Q

Quintana Court	45E
Quintana Dr.	45E,50A

R

Randall	29C
Reagor Way	49E
Rice St.	47E
Rosenberg Ave.	21C
Rosewood Dr.	40C

S

San Fernando Dr.	12F
San Jacinto Dr.	12E,67B
San Luis Pass Rd.	49E
San Marino Dr.	12F
Schaper St.	45E
Sealy St.	19E,20D
Sealy St.	21C,22B
(Ave. I)	23A,29A
Seawall E. Blvd.	3B,12D
Seawall E. Blvd.	13A
Seawall Blvd.	22D,23A
	32B,33A
	40D,41B
	42A,47D

Seawall Blvd	48B,50C
	51A
Seawolf Pkw.	1A,8A
	9A
Sherman Blvd.	41A
Sias Drive	41A
Sidney St.	39C
Skipper St.	35E
Sky Lane	35F
Skymaster Rd	38C
South Drive	48A
South Shore Dr	28F
South Jetty Rd	4A,5C
(Boddeker Drive)	
St. Mary's Blvd.	11F,22B
(8th St.)	
Stewart Rd.	29E,39B
	40A,45E
	46E,47C
	48A,49C
	50A
Strand St.	11E,21A
Suhler Rd	9D
Swan Dr.	40D
Sycamore Dr.	38D,39C
Sydnor Lane	45D

T

Tarpon Ave.	12A
Teal Dr.	40D
Teichman Rd.	24F,25E
Terminal Dr.	37D,46B
Texas Ave.	11F,12E
Todd St.	9B,10C
Tradewinds	45E
Travel Air Rd.	35D,36E
(99th St.)	45A
Travis Drive	29D
Tremont St.	21A,32B
(23rd St.)	
Trout Ave.	12A
Tuna Ave.	12C
Turn Dr.	40C

U

University Blvd.	12F,23A
Ursuline St.	21E,22E
Ursuline St.	30B,31A
(Ave. N)	32A

Street Location

V

Victory Ave.	39A

W

Walsh Lane	26C
Water St.	10F,11E
(Ave. A)	12E,20B
	21A
Weber Ave.	40E
Weis Dr.	48A
West Dansby Dr.	48A
Westwood	40D
Wharton Ave.	29D
Whiting Ave.	12A
Williams Dr.	48A
Williamsburg Dr.	39A
Willow Lane	39A
Wilnox St.	27D
Wimcrest St.	39C
Winnie St.	18F,19E
(Ave. G)	20C,21B
	22A,23A
	29A
Woodrow Ave.	41A

Y

Yale St.		47E
Yucca Dr.	38F,39C	
Yupon		39E

NUMBERED STREETS

1st St.		12E
2nd St.		12A,23A
3rd St.		12E,23A
4th St.		*12C,23A*
(Holiday Drive)		
5th St.		11F,12E
5th St.		23A
6th St.		23A
(University Blvd.)		
7 Mile Rd		49D,50C
7th St.		22B,23A
7 1/2 Mile Rd		49D
8 Mile Rd		49E
(Anderson Ways Road)		

8th St.		11F,22B
9th St.		11F,22B
10th St.		11F,22B
(Bertolino's View)		
11th St.		11E,22A
12th St.		11E,22A
13th St.		11E,22A
(Chataignon Place)		
14th St.		22A
(Christopher Columbus Blvd.)		
15th St.		22A
16th St.		21B,22A
17th St.		21B,22C
17th St.		33A
18th St.		21B,22E
		33A
19th St.		21B,33A
20th St.		21A,32B
21st St.		21A,32B
(Moody Ave.)		
22nd St.	21A,32B	
(Kempner)		
23rd St.		21A,32B
(Tremont St.)		
24th St.		21A,32A
25th St.		21A,32A
26th St.		20B,21C
		32A
27th St.		20B,21E
		32A
28th St.		20B,28A
		32A
29th St.		20B,31B
(Martin Luther King Blvd.)		32C
30th St.		20D,31B
		32C
31st St.		20F,31B
32nd St.	20C,31B	
33rd St.		20C,31A
34th St.	20C,31A	
35th St.		20C,31A
36th St.		19F,20E
		31A
37th St.		19F,31A
38th St.		19F,30B
		31C
39th St.		19F,30B
(Mike Gaido Blvd.)		31C,42A

THE CITY

40th St.	19F,30B 31E	61st St.	28A,39B 40C
41st St.	19E,30B 41B	62nd St.	28C
42nd St.	19E,30B 41B	63rd St.	28C
43rd St.	19E,30A 41B	64th St.	27D,28C
44th St.	19E,30A	65th St.	39A
45th St.	19E,30A 41B	67th St.	39A
46th St.	18F,30A 41A	68th St.	38B,39C
47th St.	29B,30C 41A	69th St.	38B,48B
48th St.	18F,29B 30C,41A	71st St.	27A,38D
49th St.	29B,30E 41A	72nd St.	38D
		73rd St.	38B
		74th St.	38D,48A
		(Pine St.)	
50th St.	29B,40B 41A	75th St.	48A
51st St.	18E,29A 40B	77th St.	26A,47B
52nd St.	29A,40B	79th St.	47D
53rd St.	18E,29A		
(Mary Moody Northen)	40D	80th St.	47D
54th St.	18E,29A 40B	81st St.	47A
55th St.	29A,40A	*(Jones Drive)*	
56th St.	29C,40A	83rd St.	37F,47A
57th St.	28D,29C 40A	85th St.	25F,47E
59th St.	28A,39B 40A	87th St.	46F,47E
(Leonard Ave.)		89th St.	25C,46F
		(Blume St.)	51B
		91st St.	25C
		93rd St.	24F
		99th St.	45A
		(Travel Air Rd)	
		103rd St.	45C
		(Anderson Ways Road)	

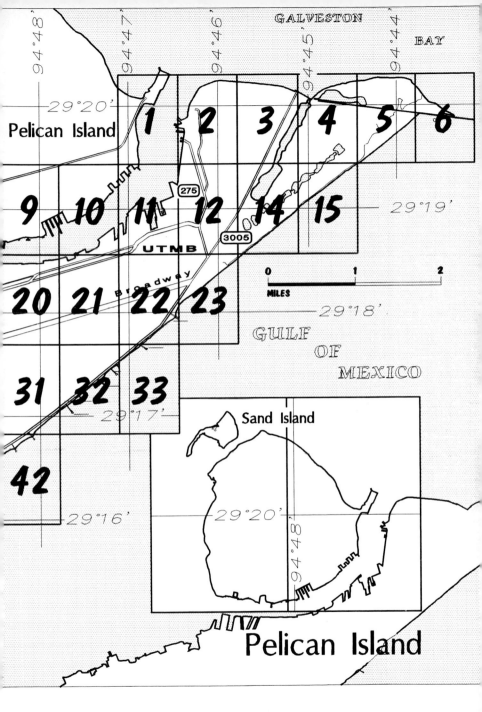

KEY TO MAP PAGES

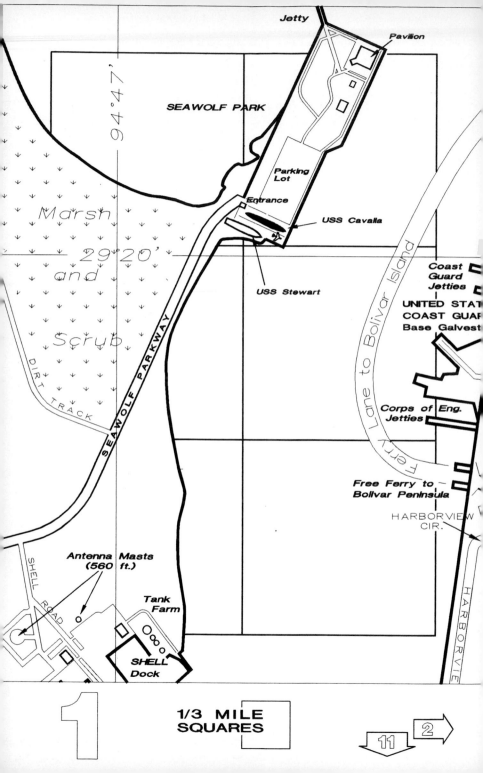

Jetty

Pavilion

SEAWOLF PARK

94°47'

Parking
Lot

Entrance

USS Cavalla

USS Stewart

Marsh

29°20'

and

Scrub

DIRT TRACK

SEAWOLF PARKWAY

Coast
Guard
Jetties

UNITED STAT
COAST GUAR
Base Galvest

Ferry Lane to Bolivar Island

Corps of Eng.
Jetties

Free Ferry to
Bolivar Peninsula

HARBORVIE
CIR.

HARBORVIE

Antenna Masts
(560 ft.)

Tank
Farm

SHELL ROAD

SHELL
Dock

1

1/3 MILE
SQUARES

11

2

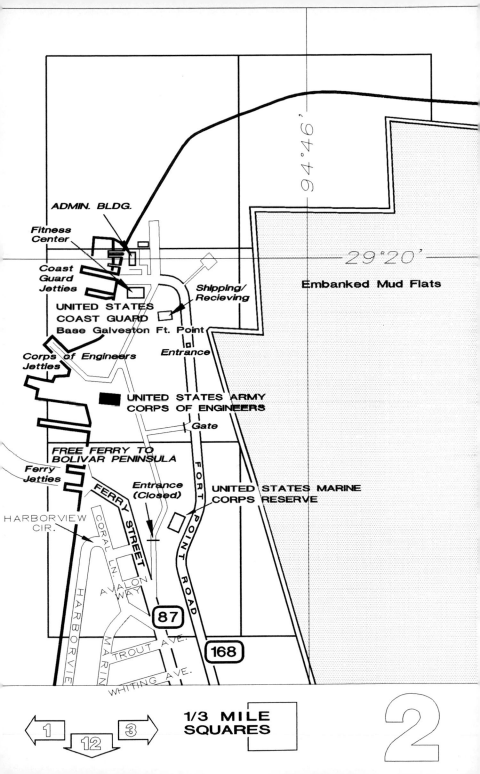

ADMIN. BLDG.

Fitness
Center

Coast
Guard
Jetties

UNITED STATES
COAST GUARD
Base Galveston Ft. Point

Corps of Engineers
Jetties

Shipping/
Recieving

Entrance

UNITED STATES ARMY
CORPS OF ENGINEERS

Gate

FREE FERRY TO
BOLIVAR PENINSULA

Ferry
Jetties

Entrance
(Closed)

UNITED STATES MARINE
CORPS RESERVE

HARBORVIEW
CIR.

FERRY STREET

CORAL LN.

AVALON WAY

HARBORVIE

MARIN

TROUT AVE.

WHITING AVE.

FORT POINT ROAD

87

168

94°46'

29°20'

Embanked Mud Flats

1/3 MILE
SQUARES

1

12

3

2

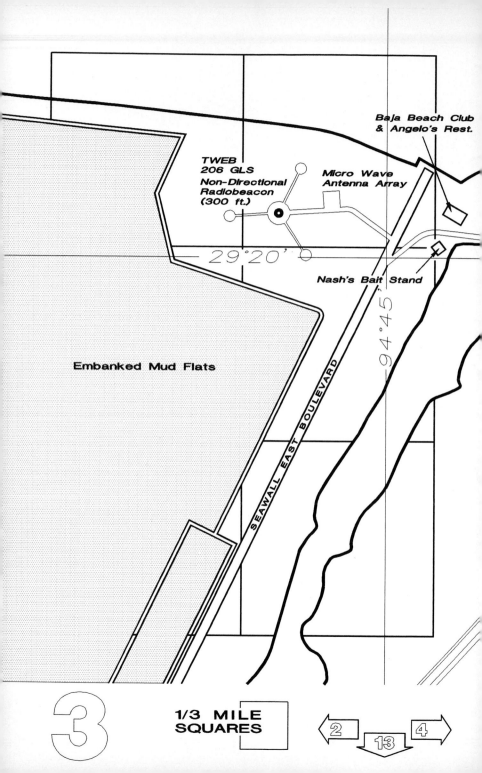

Baja Beach Club
& Angelo's Rest.

**TWEB
206 GLS
Non-Directional
Radiobeacon
(300 ft.)**

*Micro Wave
Antenna Array*

29°20'

94°45'

Nash's Bait Stand

Embanked Mud Flats

SEAWALL EAST BOULEVARD

3

**1/3 MILE
SQUARES**

2 13 4

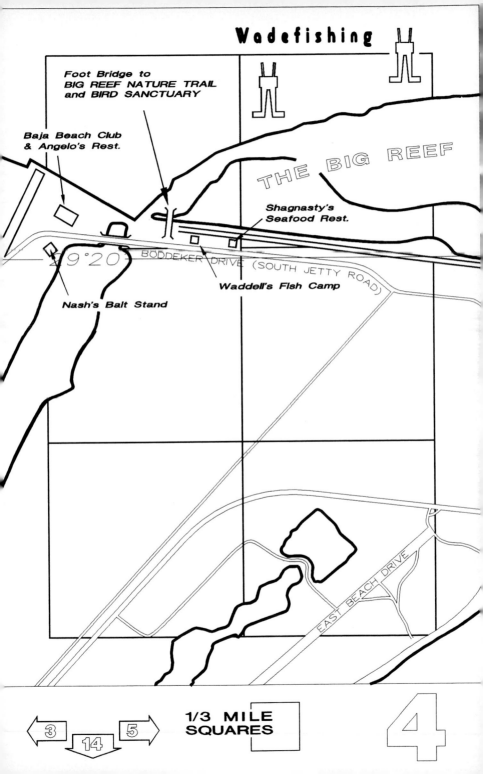

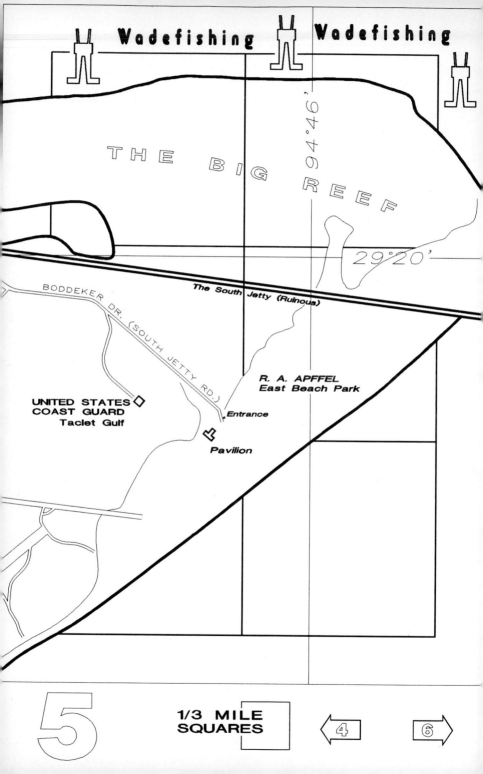

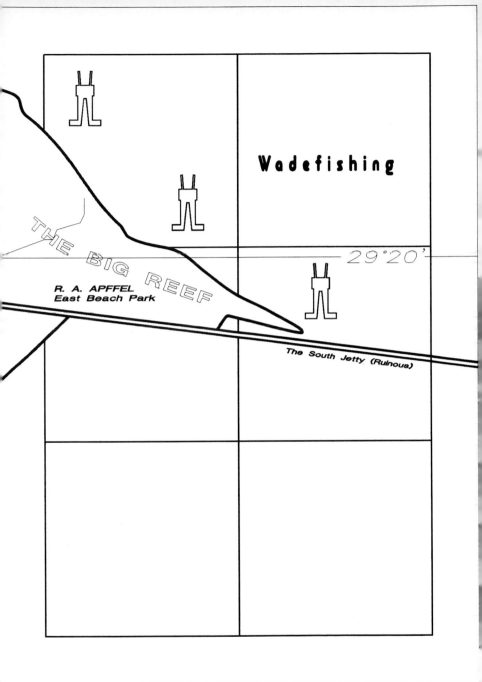

Wadefishing

29°20'

THE BIG REEF

R. A. APFFEL
East Beach Park

The South Jetty (Ruinous)

‹5

1/3 MILE
SQUARES

6

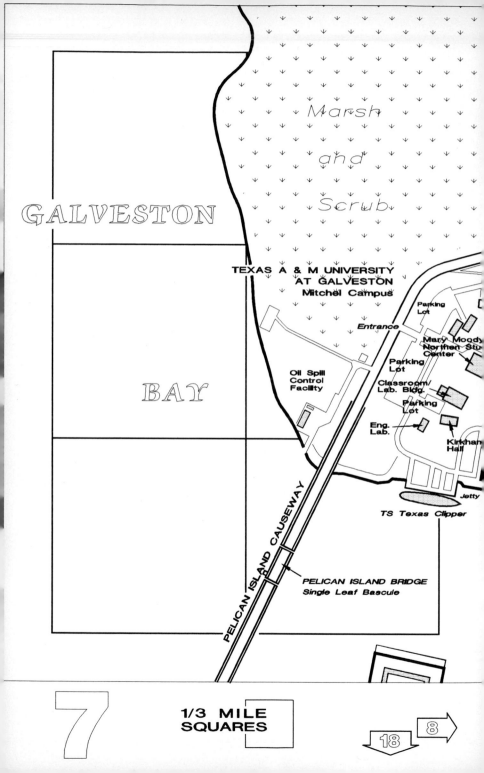

MARSH
and
Scrub

GALVESTON

TEXAS A & M UNIVERSITY
AT GALVESTON
Mitchel Campus

Parking
Lot

Entrance

Mary Moody
Northen Stu
Center

Parking
Lot

BAY

Oil Spill
Control
Facility

Classroom/
Lab. Bldg.

Parking
Lot

Eng.
Lab.

Kinkhan
Hall

Jetty

TS Texas Clipper

PELICAN ISLAND CAUSEWAY

PELICAN ISLAND BRIDGE
Single Leaf Bascule

7

1/3 MILE
SQUARES

18 8

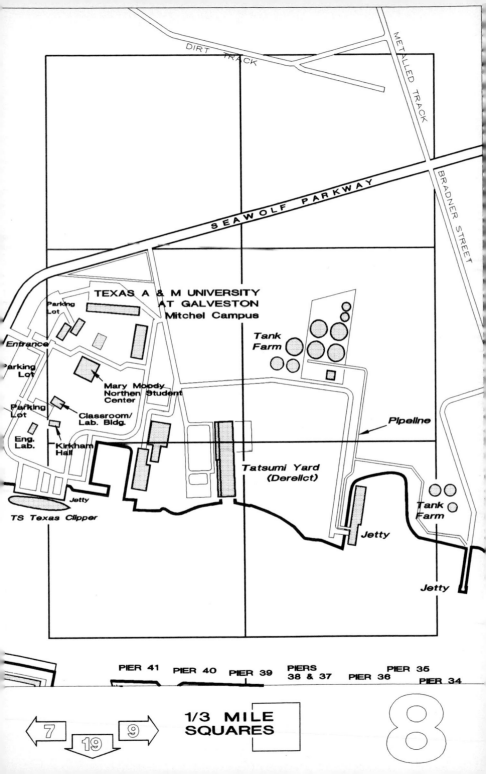

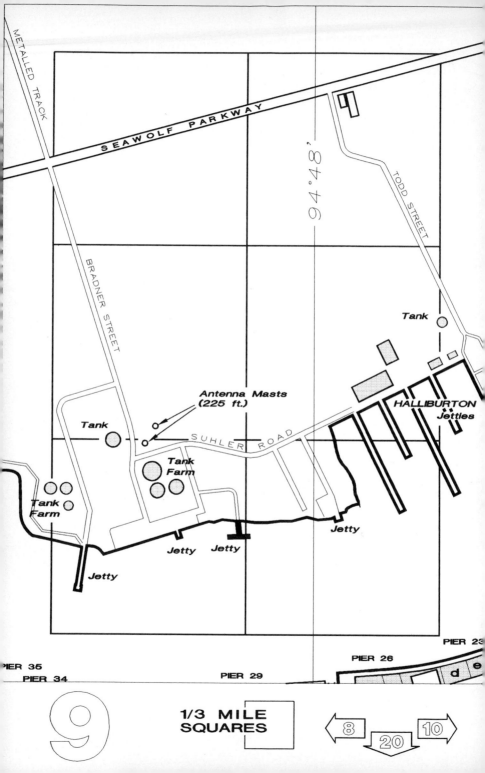

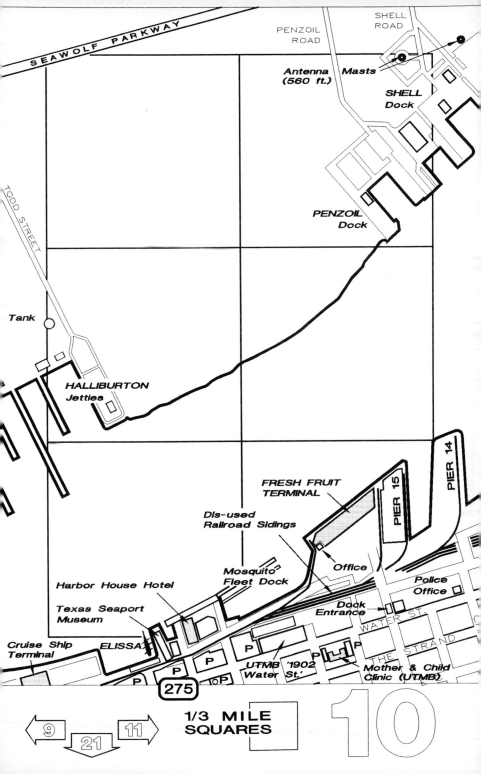

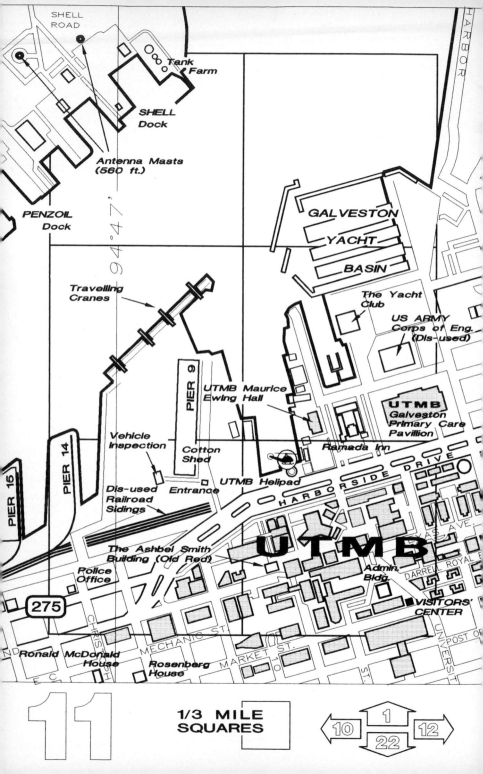

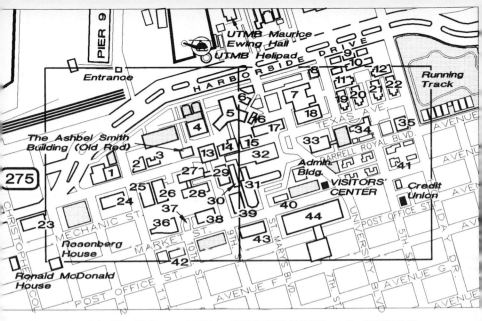

UTMB

THE UNVERSITY of TEXAS
MEDICAL BRANCH at GALVESTON

1 Pathology Building
2 Mary Moody Northern Pavilion
3 Marvin Graves Building
4 Emergency & Trauma Dept.
5 Texas Department of Criminal Justice Hospital
6 Services Building
7 Surgical Research Building
8 Physical Plant
9 Medical Engineering
10 Nolan Hall
11 Clay Hall
12 Morgan Hall
13 University Hospital Clinics
14 John W. McCullough Building
15 John Sealy Surgical Annex
16 Communications Building
17 Jennie Sealy Hospital
18 Former Shriners Burns Building
19 Brackenridge Hall
20 Bethel Hall
21 Vinsant Hall
22 League Hall
23 Materials Managemt. Warehse.
24 Allied Health Sciences and Nursing Building

25 Medical Research Building
26 Libbie Moody Thompson Basic Science Building
27 Kieller Building
28 Gall Borden Building
29 Clinical Sciences Building
30 Old Childrens' Hospital
31 John Sealy Tower
32 John Sealy Hospital
33 Sealy & Smith Prof. Bldg.
34 Family Medicine/ Geriatric Day Hospital
35 Alumini Field House and Swimming Pool
36 William C. Levin Hall
37 Gleaves T. James Centennial Rose Garden
38 Moody Medical Library
39 Childrens' Hospital
40 Administration Annex
41 The Residence
42 Pharmacology Building
43 Shriners Burns Institute
44 St. Mary's Hospital

1/3 MILE SQUARES

UTMB

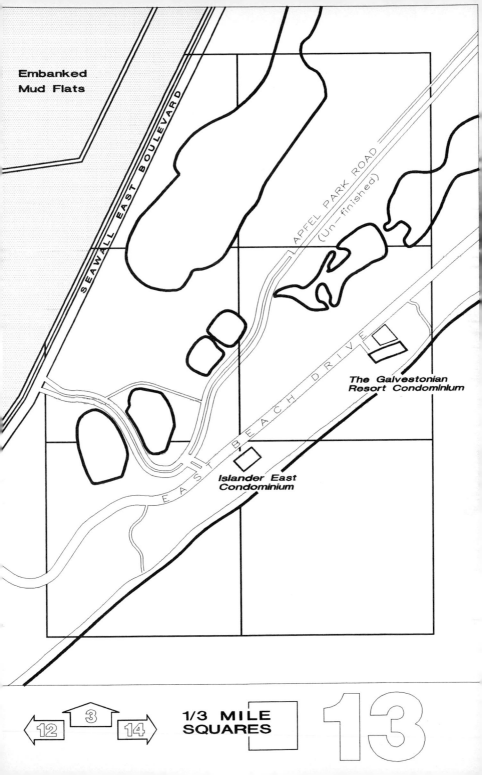

Embanked
Mud Flats

SEAWALL EAST BOULEVARD

LAPFEL PARK ROAD
(Un–finished)

EAST BEACH DRIVE

The Galvestonian
Resort Condominium

Islander East
Condominium

12 3 14

1/3 MILE
SQUARES

13

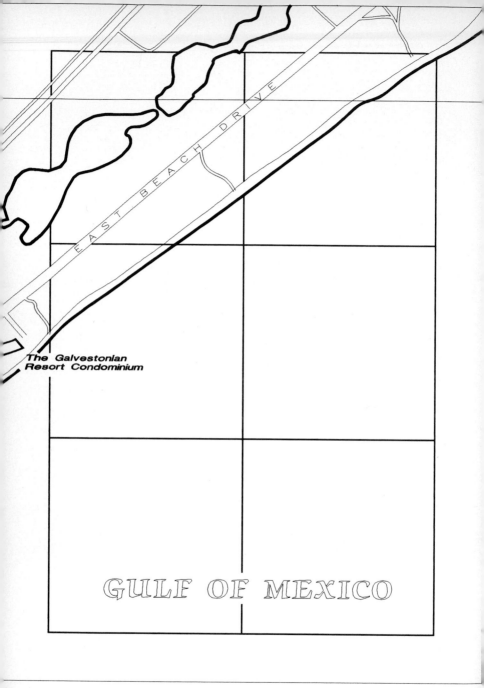

EAST BEACH DRIVE

The Galvestonian
Resort Condominium

GULF OF MEXICO

14 1/3 MILE
SQUARES

13 4

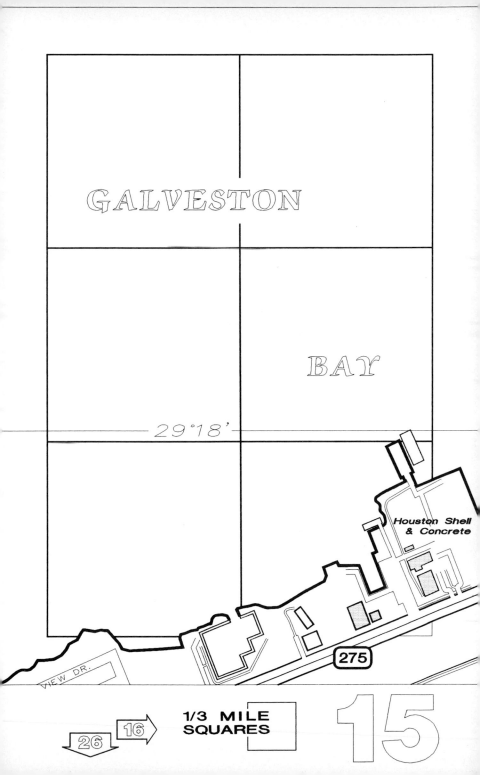

GALVESTON

BAY

29°18'

Houston Shell
& Concrete

275

VIEW DR.

26 16

1/3 MILE
SQUARES

15

GALVESTON

BAY

94°51'

29°18'

Texas Gulf
Construction

American Fence
& Supply Co.

Dry Dock   Dry Dock

Galveston Shipbuilding
Co.

Houston Shell
& Concrete

HARBORSIDE DRIVE

LBCO Inc.

VEHICLE EMMISSIONS
INSPECTION STATION

275

Lone Star
Rest. Equip. Co.

16   1/3 MILE
          SQUARES

15   27   17

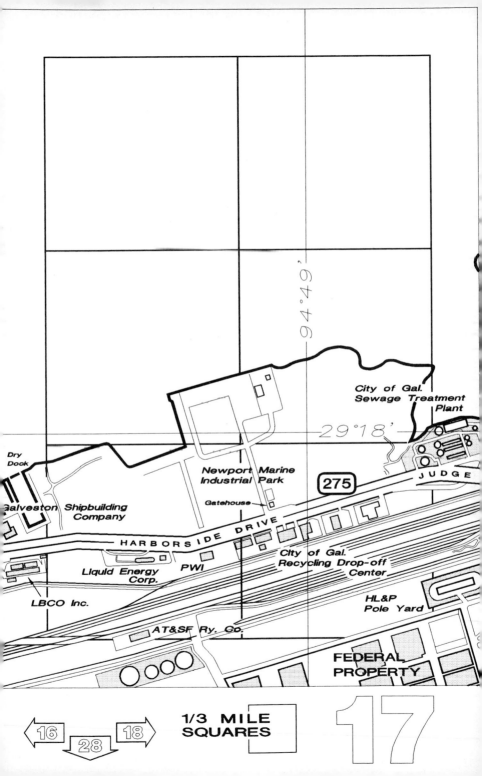

94°49'

City of Gal.
Sewage Treatment
Plant

29°18'

Dry
Dock

Newport Marine
Industrial Park

275

JUDGE

Gatehouse

Galveston Shipbuilding
Company

HARBORSIDE DRIVE

City of Gal.
Recycling Drop-off
Center

Liquid Energy
Corp.

PWI

LBCO Inc.

HL&P
Pole Yard

AT&SF Ry. Co.

FEDERAL
PROPERTY

16   18
28

1/3 MILE
SQUARES

17

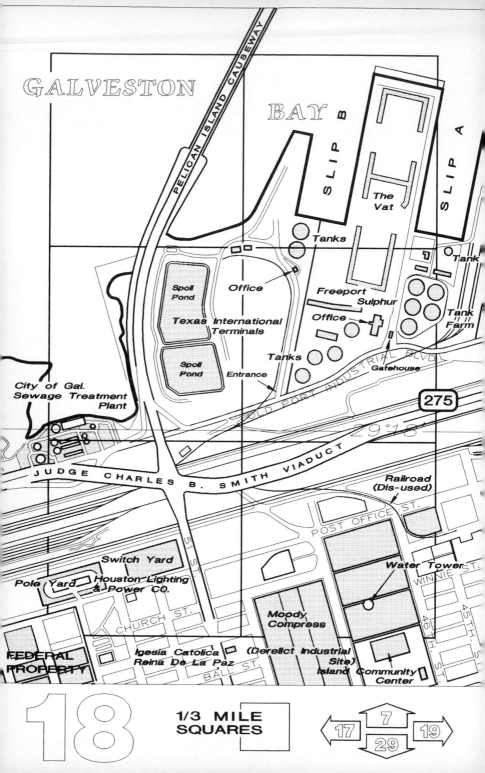

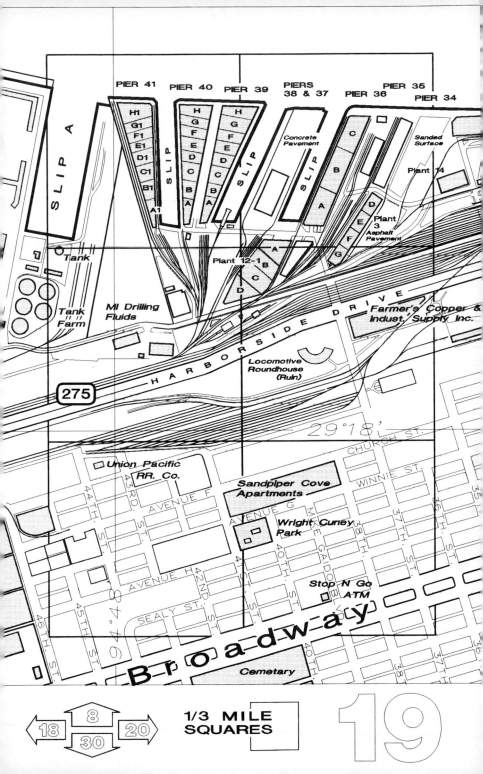

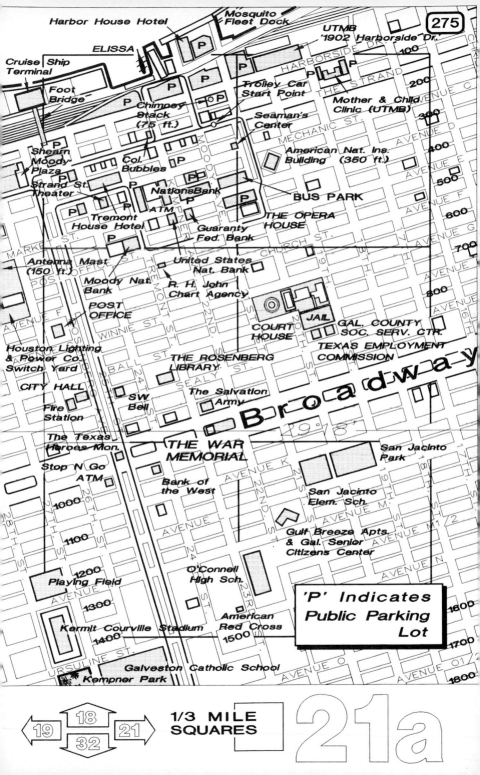

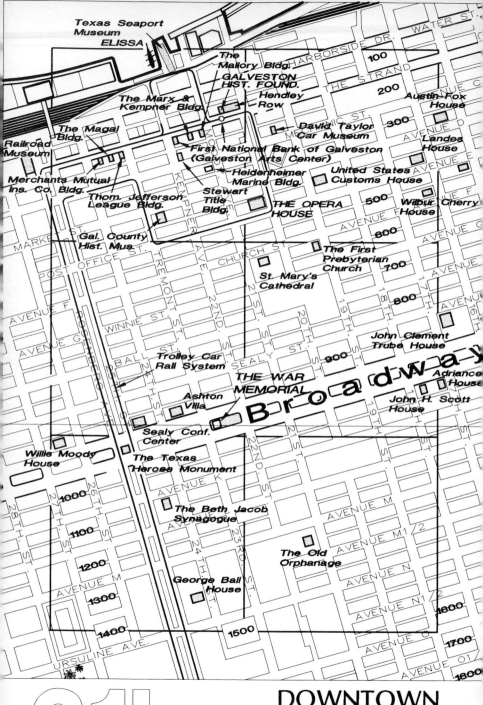

Texas Seaport
Museum
ELISSA

WATER ST.

The
Mallory Bldg.
GALVESTON
HIST. FOUND.

HARBORSIDE DR.

100

200

THE STRAND

Hendley
Row

Austin-Fox
House

The Marx &
Kempner Bldg.

David Taylor
Car Museum

300

AVENUE D

Landes
House

The Magel
Bldg.

Railroad
Museum

First National Bank of Galveston
(Galveston Arts Center)

Heidenheimer
Marine Bldg.

United States
Customs House

AVENUE E

Merchants Mutual
Ins. Co. Bldg.

Thom. Jefferson
League Bldg.

Stewart
Title
Bldg.

THE OPERA
HOUSE

500

Wilbur Cherry
House

AVENUE F

Gal. County
Hist. Mus.

AVENUE G

600

MARKET

POST OFFICE ST.

CHURCH ST.

The First
Prebytery
Church

700

AVENUE H

St. Mary's
Cathedral

800

AVENUE F

WINNIE ST.

22ND ST.

AVENUE G

John Clement
Trube House

Trolley Car
Rail System

SEALY

900

Broadway

Adriance
House

Ashton
Villa

THE WAR
MEMORIAL

John H. Scott
House

Sealy Conf.
Center

Willie Moody
House

The Texas
Heroes Monument

AVENUE K

1000

1100

The Beth Jacob
Synagogue

AVENUE M

1200

The Old
Orphanage

AVENUE M 1/2

1300

George Ball
House

AVENUE N

1600

AVENUE N 1/2

1400

1500

1700

URSULINE AVE.

AVENUE O

1800

DOWNTOWN
HISTORICAL
BUILDINGS

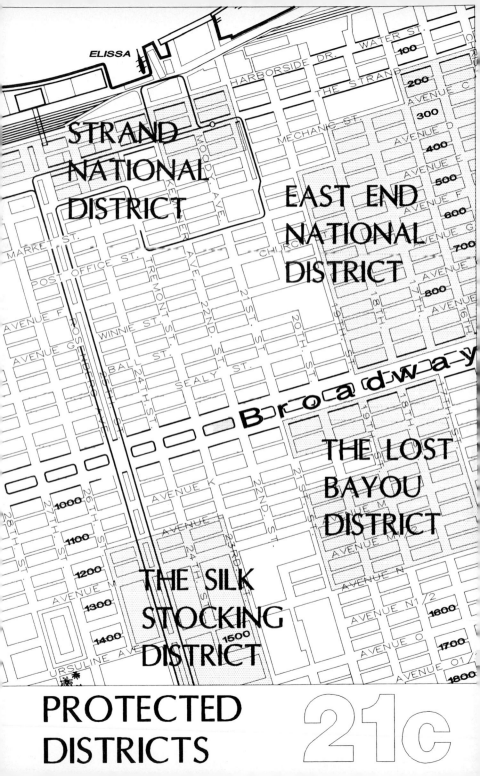

ELISSA

STRAND
NATIONAL
DISTRICT

EAST END
NATIONAL
DISTRICT

THE LOST
BAYOU
DISTRICT

THE SILK
STOCKING
DISTRICT

Broadway

PROTECTED
DISTRICTS

21c

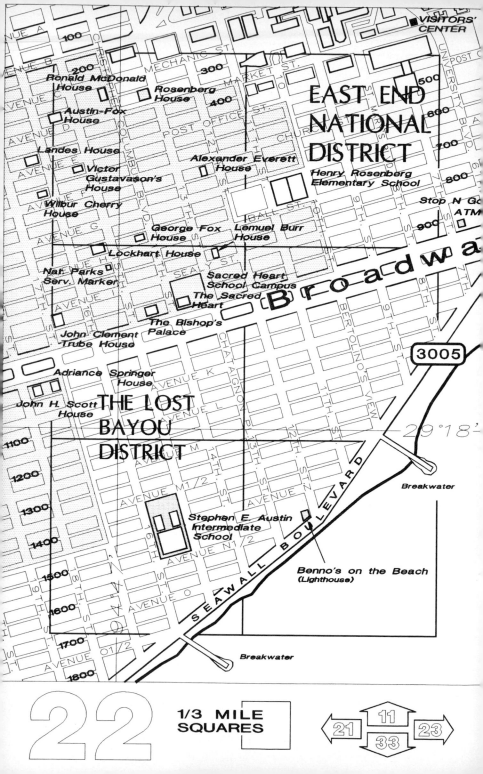

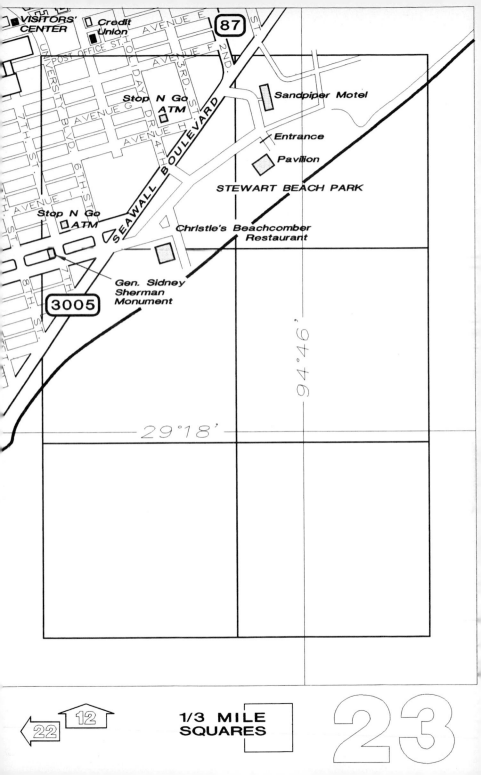

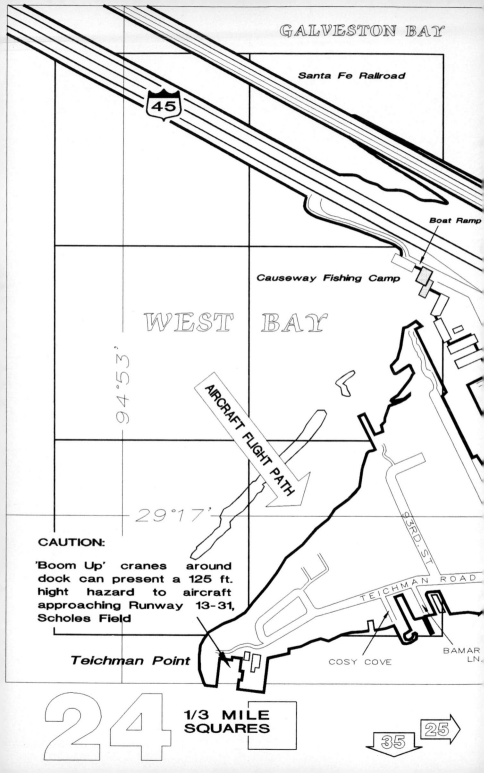

GALVESTON BAY

Santa Fe Railroad

45

Boat Ramp

Causeway Fishing Camp

WEST BAY

94°53'

AIRCRAFT FLIGHT PATH

29°17'

CAUTION:

'Boom Up' cranes around dock can present a 125 ft. hight hazard to aircraft approaching Runway 13-31, Scholes Field

93RD. ST

TEICHMAN ROAD

COSY COVE

BAMAR LN.

Teichman Point

24 1/3 MILE SQUARES

35 25

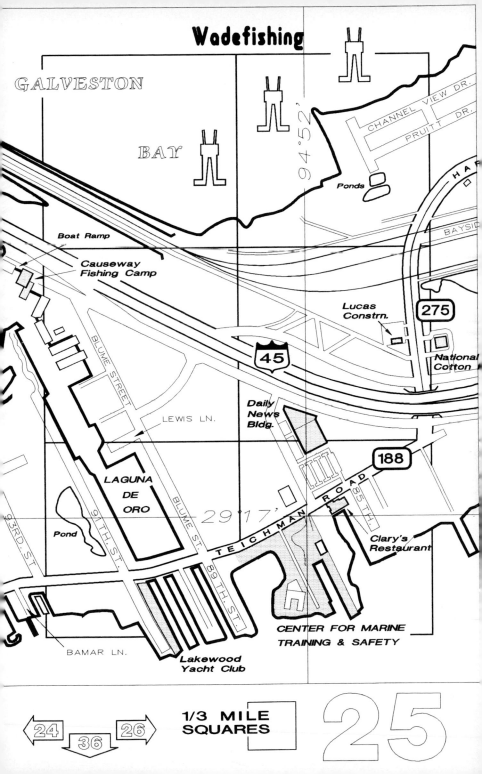

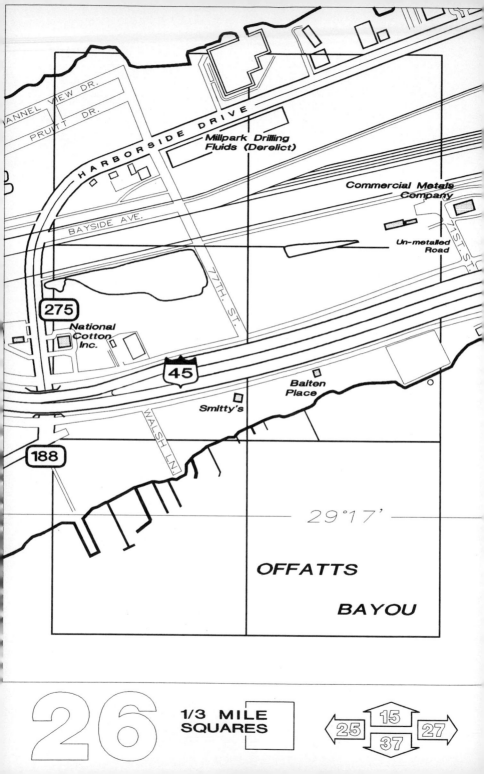

HANNEL VIEW DR.

PRUITT DR.

HARBORSIDE DRIVE

Millpark Drilling
Fluids (Derelict)

Commercial Metals
Company

BAYSIDE AVE.

Un-metalled
Road

71ST ST.

77TH ST.

275

National
Cotton
Inc.

45

Balten
Place

Smitty's

WALSH LN.

188

29°17'

OFFATTS

BAYOU

26   1/3 MILE
     SQUARES

25   15
     37   27

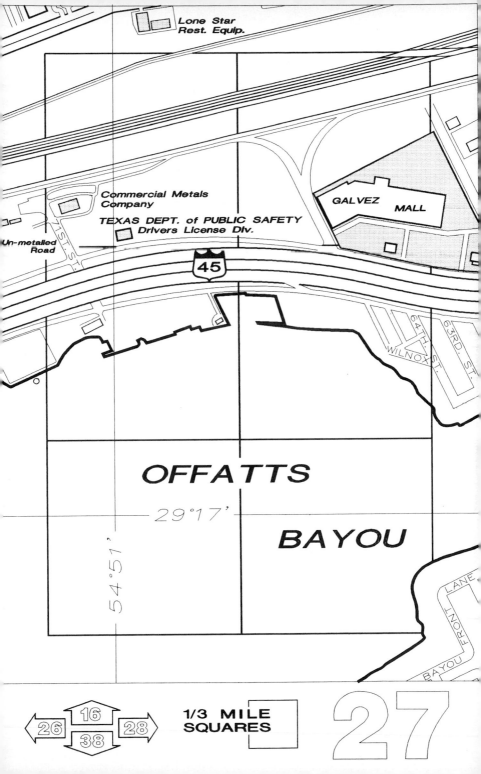

Lone Star
Rest. Equip.

Commercial Metals
Company

TEXAS DEPT. of PUBLIC SAFETY
Drivers License Div.

GALVEZ
MALL

Un-metalled
Road

71ST. ST.

45

64TH. ST.

63RD. ST.

WILNOX. ST.

OFFATTS

29°17'

BAYOU

54°51'

FRONT LANE

BAYOU

16
26   28
38

1/3 MILE
SQUARES

27

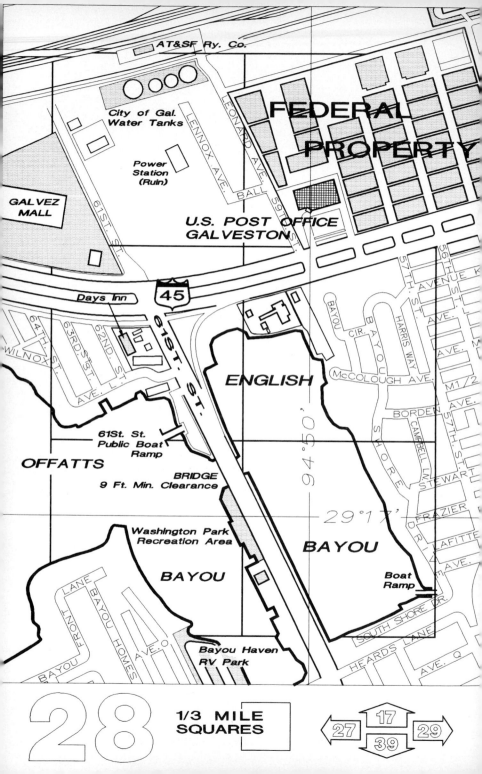

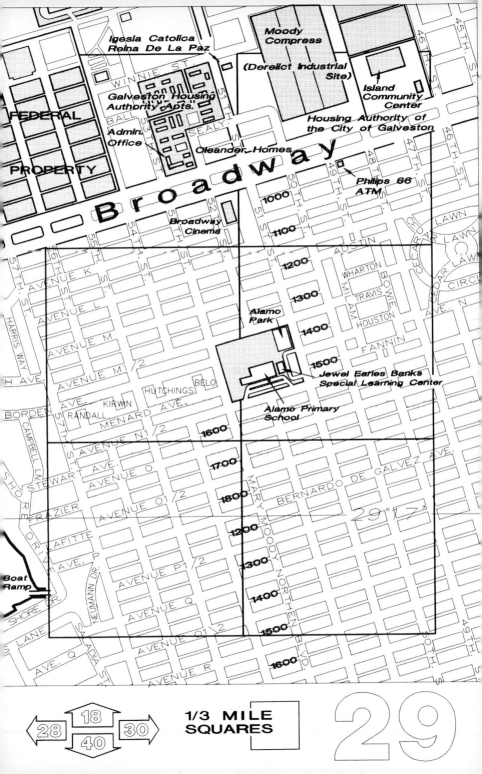

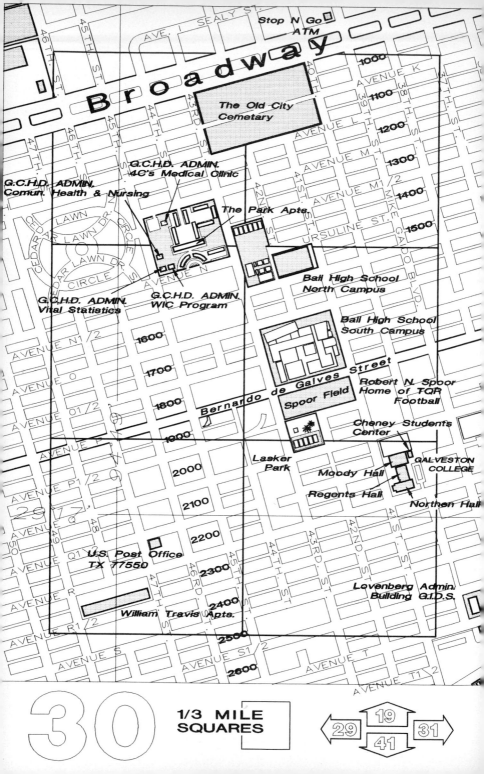

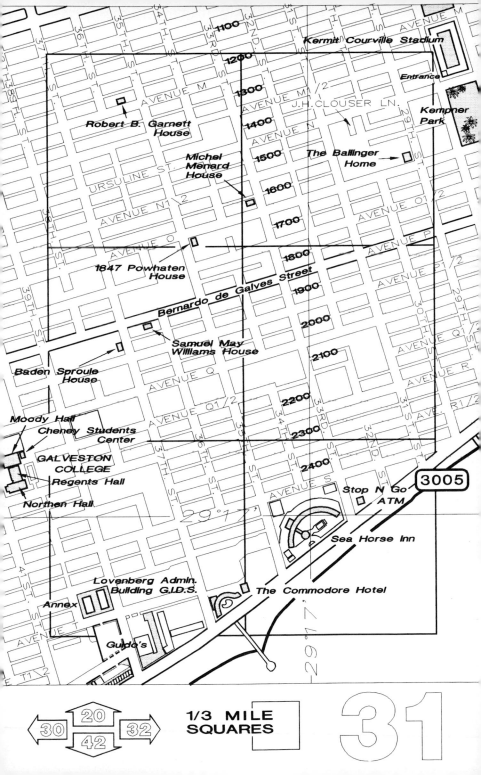

Kermit Courville Stadium

Entrance

Kempner Park

1100

1200

1300

AVENUE M 1/2

J. H. CLOUSER LN.

AVENUE M

Robert B. Garnett House

1400

AVENUE N

Michel Menard House

1500

The Ballinger Home

URSULINE ST.

1600

AVENUE N 1/2

1700

AVENUE O

1800

AVENUE O 1/2

1847 Powhaten House

Bernardo de Galves Street

1900

2000

Samuel May Williams House

2100

Baden Sproule House

AVENUE Q

AVENUE R

2200

AVENUE Q 1/2

AVENUE Q 1/2

2300

AVENUE R 1/2

Moody Hall

Cheney Students Center

GALVESTON COLLEGE

2400

Regents Hall

Northen Hall

3005

Stop N Go ATM

29° 17'

Sea Horse Inn

Lovenberg Admin. Building G.I.D.S.

Annex

The Commodore Hotel

29° 17'

Guido's

AVENUE T 1/2

20

30   32

42

1/3 MILE SQUARES

31

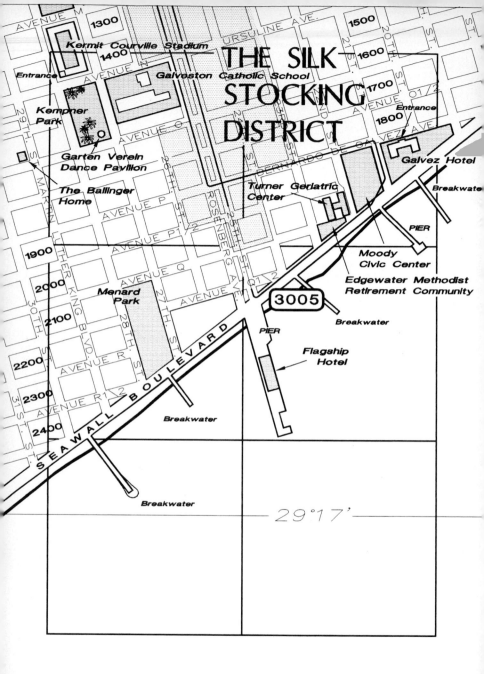

AVENUE M
1300
Kermit Courville Stadium
1400
Entrance
Galveston Catholic School
URSULINE AVE.
1500
1600
THE SILK
STOCKING
DISTRICT
1700
Entrance
1800

AVENUE N

AVENUE O

Kempner Park

Garten Verein Dance Pavilion

The Ballinger Home

Galvez Hotel

Breakwater

Turner Geriatric Center

AVENUE P

AVENUE P1/2

1900

Moody Civic Center

PIER

Edgewater Methodist Retirement Community

2000

AVENUE Q

Menard Park

AVENUE Q1/2

3005

Breakwater

2100

PIER

Flagship Hotel

2200

AVENUE R

2300

AVENUE R1/2

2400

Breakwater

SEAWALL BOULEVARD

Breakwater

29°17'

32   1/3 MILE SQUARES   ←31 21 33→

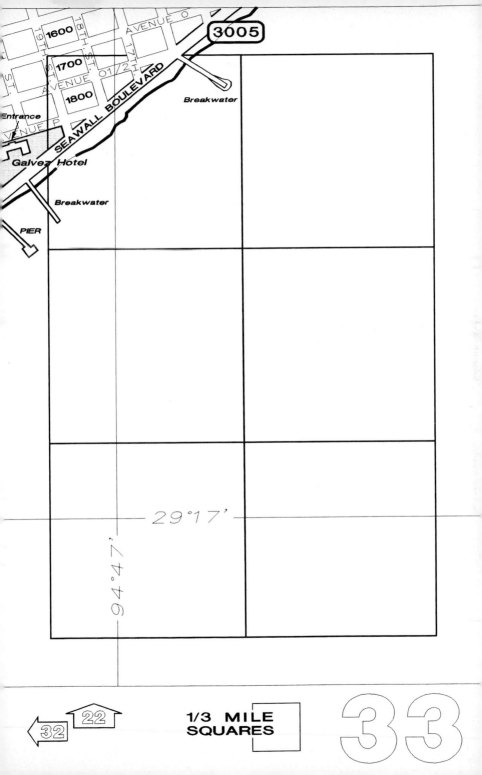

1600
1700
1800
AVENUE O
AVENUE
AVENUE P
3005
SEAWALL BOULEVARD
Breakwater
Entrance
Galvez Hotel
Breakwater
PIER

29°17'

94°47'

32   22

1/3 MILE
SQUARES

33

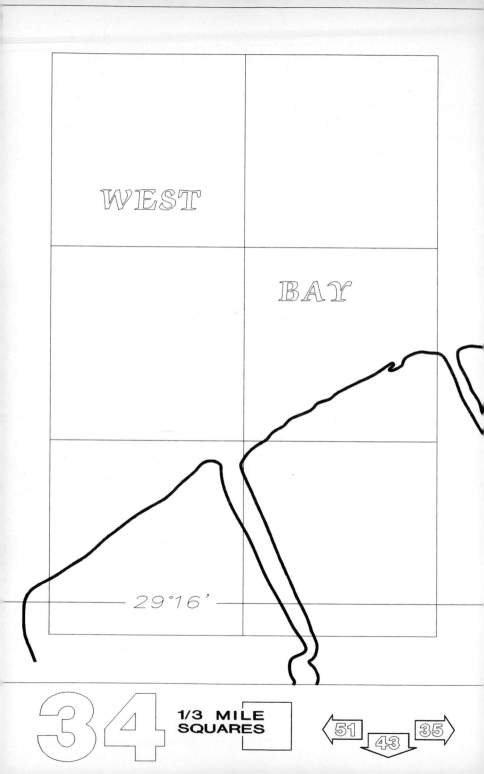

WEST

BAY

29°16'

34 1/3 MILE
SQUARES

◁51 43▽ 35▷

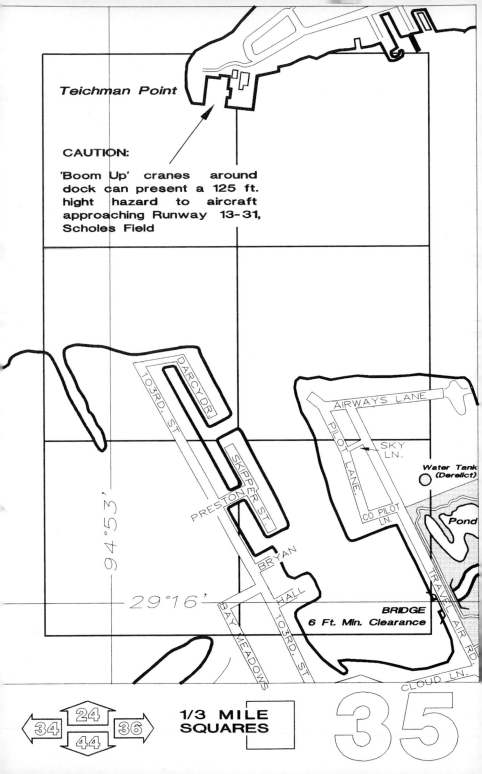

Teichman Point

CAUTION:

'Boom Up' cranes around dock can present a 125 ft. hight hazard to aircraft approaching Runway 13-31, Scholes Field

DARCY DR.

103RD. ST.

AIRWAYS LANE

PILOT LANE.

SKY LN.

Water Tank (Derelict)

SKIPPER ST.

PRESTON ST.

CO PILOT LN.

Pond

94°53'

BRYAN

HALL

29°16'

BAY MEADOWS

103RD. ST.

TRAVEL AIR RD.

BRIDGE
6 Ft. Min. Clearance

CLOUD LN.

24
34 H 36
44

**1/3 MILE
SQUARES**

35

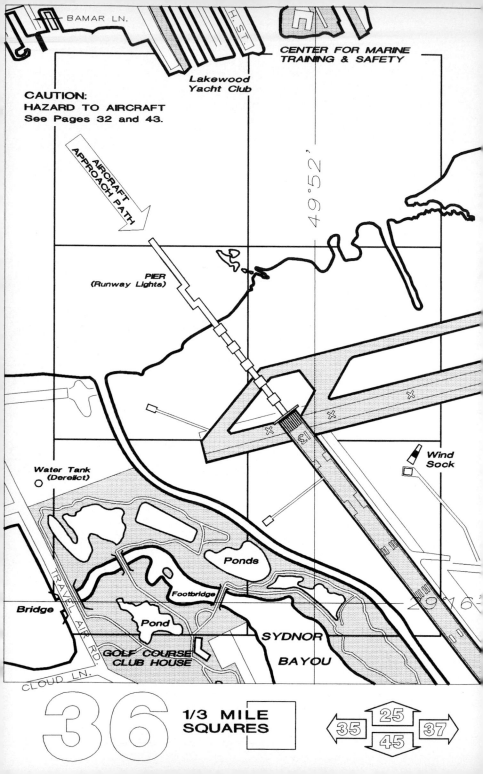

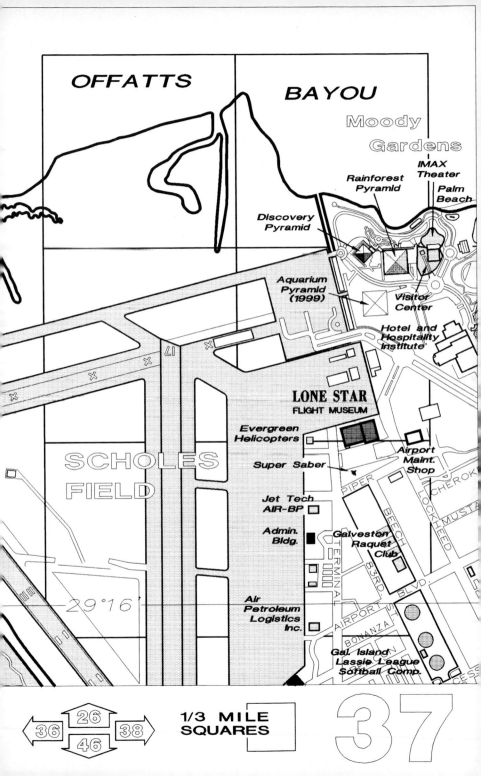

OFFATTS   BAYOU

Moody
Gardens

IMAX
Theater

Rainforest
Pyramid

Palm
Beach

Discovery
Pyramid

Aquarium
Pyramid
(1999)

Visitor
Center

Hotel and
Hospitality
Institute

LONE STAR
FLIGHT MUSEUM

Evergreen
Helicopters

Airport
Maint.
Shop

Super Saber

Jet Tech
AIR-BP

SCHOLES
FIELD

Admin.
Bldg.

Galveston
Raquet
Club

29°16'

Air
Petroleum
Logistics
Inc.

Gal. Island
Lassie League
Softball Comp.

36 ⟷ 26 / 46 ⟷ 38

1/3 MILE
SQUARES

37

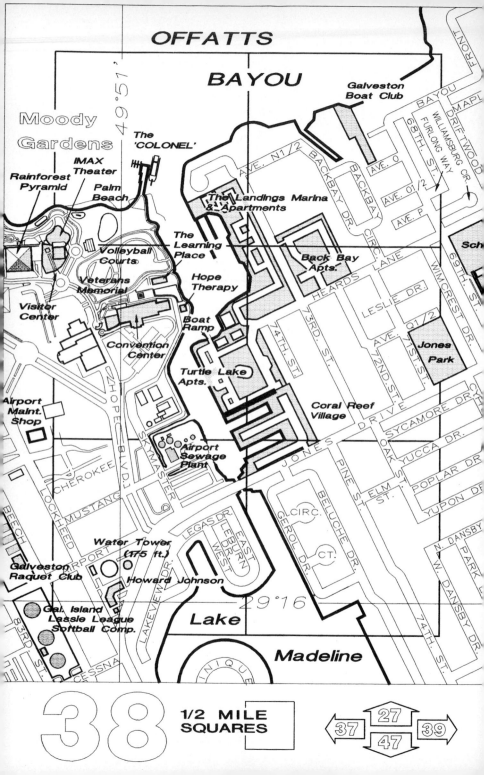

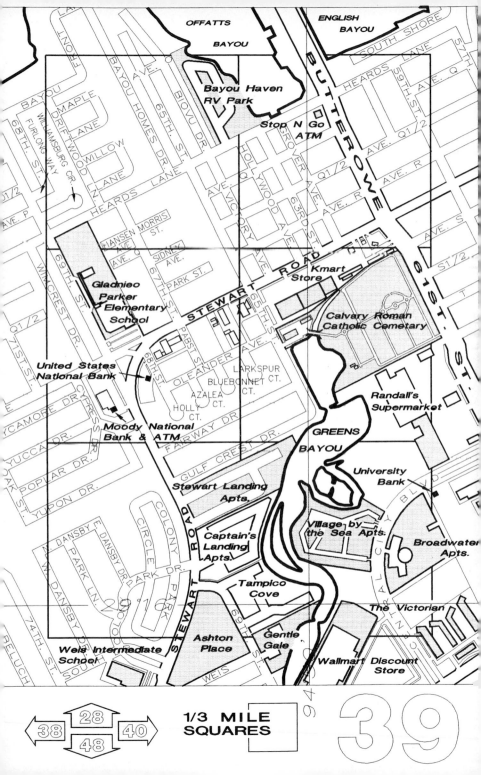

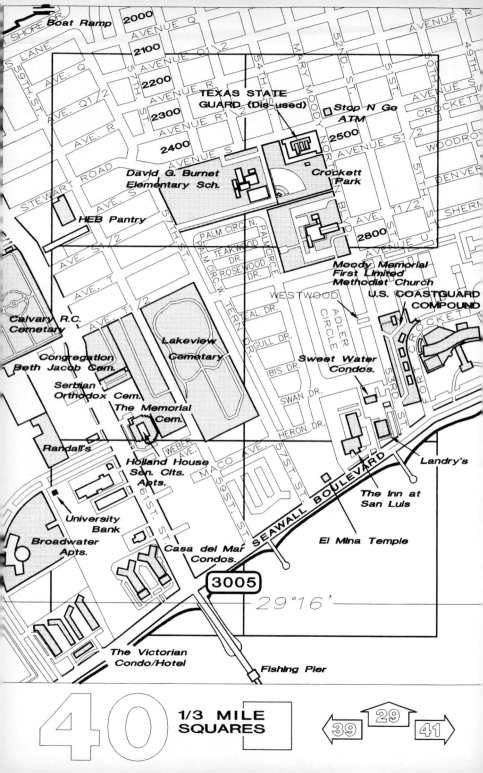

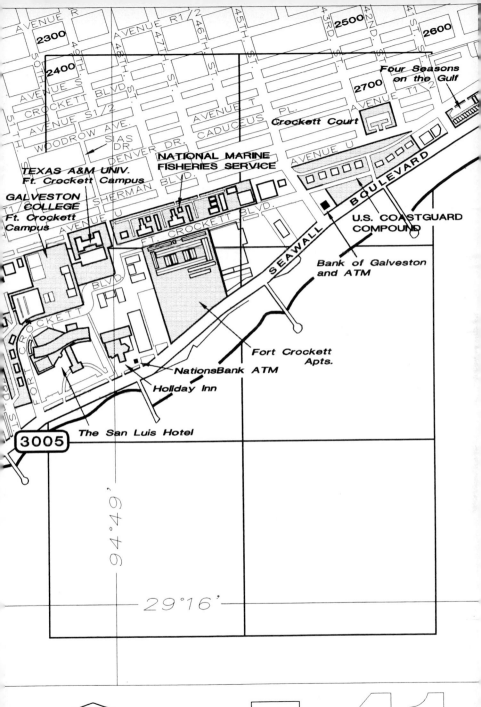

AVENUE R
2300
2400
AVENUE R1/2
2500
2600
Four Seasons on the Gulf
2700
AVENUE S
CROCKETT BLVD.
AVENUE S1/2
WOODROW AVE.
SIAS DR.
DENVER DR.
CADUCEUS
AVENUE T
Crockett Court
AVENUE T1/2
TEXAS A&M UNIV.
Ft. Crockett Campus
NATIONAL MARINE
FISHERIES SERVICE
AVENUE U
GALVESTON
COLLEGE
Ft. Crockett
Campus
SHERMAN
AVENUE U
FT. CROCKETT BLVD.
BOULEVARD
U.S. COASTGUARD
COMPOUND
FT. CROCKETT BLVD.
SEAWALL
Bank of Galveston
and ATM
Fort Crockett
Apts.
FT. CROCKETT BLVD.
NationsBank ATM
Holiday Inn
The San Luis Hotel
3005
9°46.9'
29°16'

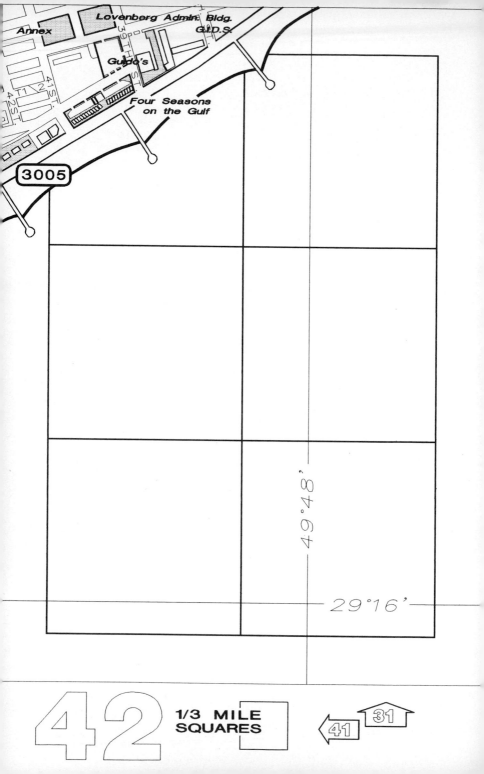

Annex

Lovenberg Admin. Bldg.
G.I.D.S.

Guido's

Four Seasons
on the Gulf

3005

49°48'

29°16'

42 1/3 MILE
SQUARES

41 31

The 3-masted barque 'Elissa', built
in 1877. Pier 21, 22nd. Street.

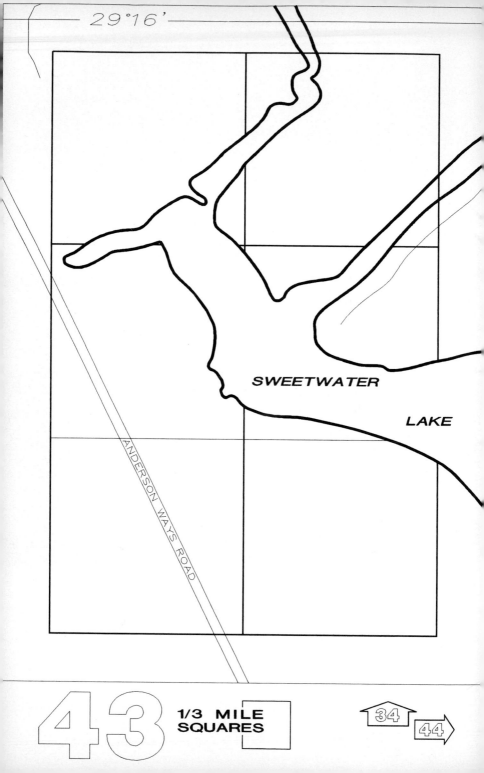

SWEETWATER

LAKE

ANDERSON WAYS ROAD

43 1/3 MILE
SQUARES

34

44

29°16'

94°53'

HALL

BAY MEADOWS

103RD. ST.

BRIDGE
6 Ft. Min. Clearance

AIR RD.

CLOUD LN.

BROOME RD.

103RD. ST.

BROOME RD.

SWEETWATER

LAKE

43 ← 35 / 49 → 45

1/3 MILE
SQUARES

44

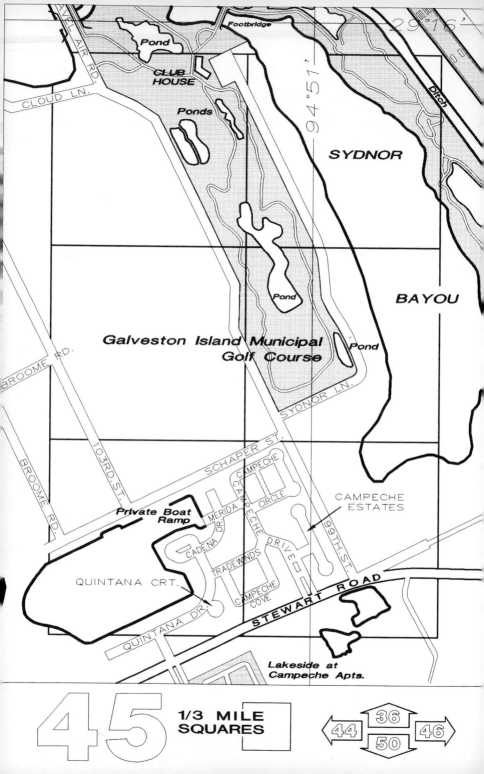

29° 16'

Footbridge

Pond

CLUB
HOUSE

CLOUD LN.

Ponds

94° 51'

SYDNOR

BAYOU

Pond

Galveston Island Municipal
Golf Course

Pond

SYDNOR LN.

Ditch

BROOME RD.

103RD. ST.

SCHAPER ST.

CAMPECHE CIRCLE

CAMPECHE
ESTATES

Private Boat
Ramp

MERIDA DR.

CADENA DR.

TRADEWINDS DRIVE

CAMPECHE DRIVE

99TH. ST.

BROOME RD.

QUINTANA CRT.

CAMPECHE
COVE

QUINTANA DR.

STEWART ROAD

Lakeside at
Campeche Apts.

45 1/3 MILE
    SQUARES

44 36 46
    50

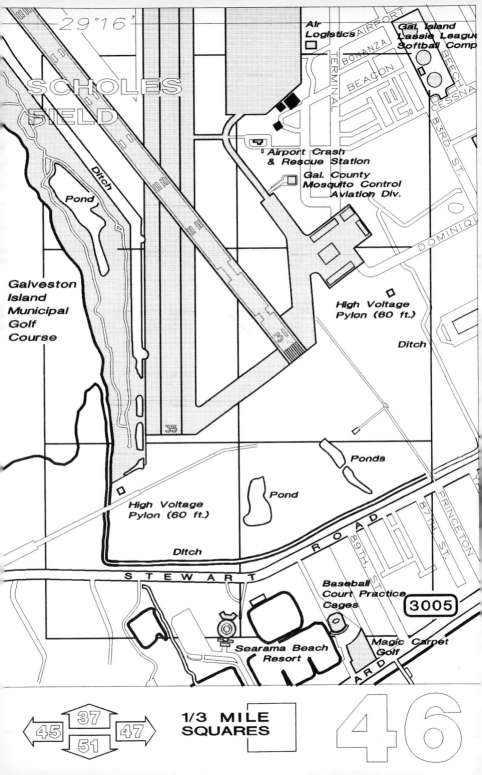

29°16'

Air Logistics

AIRPORT

BONANZA

BEACON

TERMINAL

Gal. Island Lassie League Softball Comp

BEECHA

CESSNA

B3RD. ST.

SCHOLES FIELD

Ditch

Pond

Airport Crash & Rescue Station

Gal. County Mosquito Control Aviation Div.

DOMINIQU

Galveston Island Municipal Golf Course

High Voltage Pylon (60 ft.)

Ditch

35

31

Ponds

High Voltage Pylon (60 ft.)

Pond

PRINCETON

87TH. ST.

Ditch

S T E W A R T

ROAD

89TH. ST.

Baseball Court Practice Cages

3005

Searama Beach Resort

Magic Carpet Golf

ARD

45 37 47
    51

1/3 MILE SQUARES

46

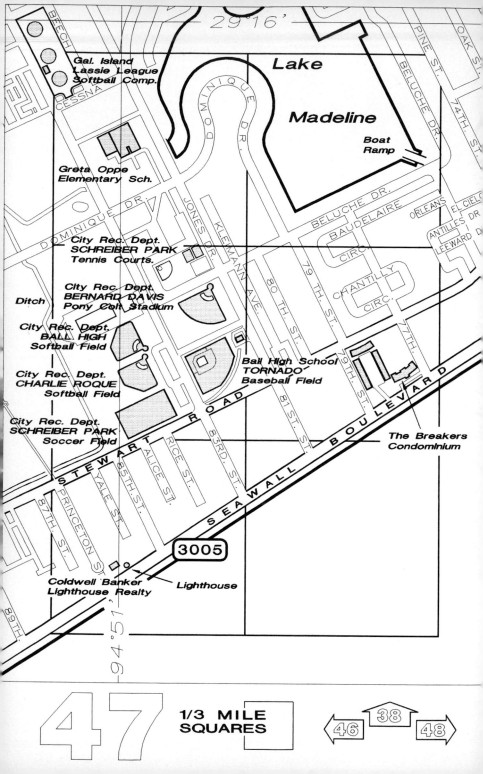

29°16'

Lake
Madeline

Gal. Island
Lassie League
Softball Comp.

BEECH

CESSNA

Boat
Ramp

PINE ST.

OAK ST.

74TH ST.

Greta Oppe
Elementary Sch.

DOMINIQUE DR.

BELUCHE DR.

BELUCHE DR.

BAUDELAIRE

ORLEANS

EL CIELO

ANTILLES DR.

LEEWARD DR.

DOMINIQUE DR.

JONES DR.

KLEMANN AVE.

City Rec. Dept.
SCHREIBER PARK
Tennis Courts.

CHANTILLY CIRC.

79 TH ST.

80 TH ST.

City Rec. Dept.
BERNARD DAVIS
Pony Colt Stadium

Ditch

City Rec. Dept.
BALL HIGH
Softball Field

City Rec. Dept.
CHARLIE ROQUE
Softball Field

77TH.

Ball High School
TORNADO
Baseball Field

79TH ST.

77TH.

City Rec. Dept.
SCHREIBER PARK
Soccer Field

STEWART ROAD

RICE ST.

83RD ST.

81 ST ST.

SEAWALL BOULEVARD

The Breakers
Condominium

ALICE ST.

85TH ST.

YALE ST.

PRINCETON ST.

87TH. ST.

3005

Coldwell Banker
Lighthouse Realty

Lighthouse

89TH.

94°51'

47 1/3 MILE
SQUARES

46   38   48

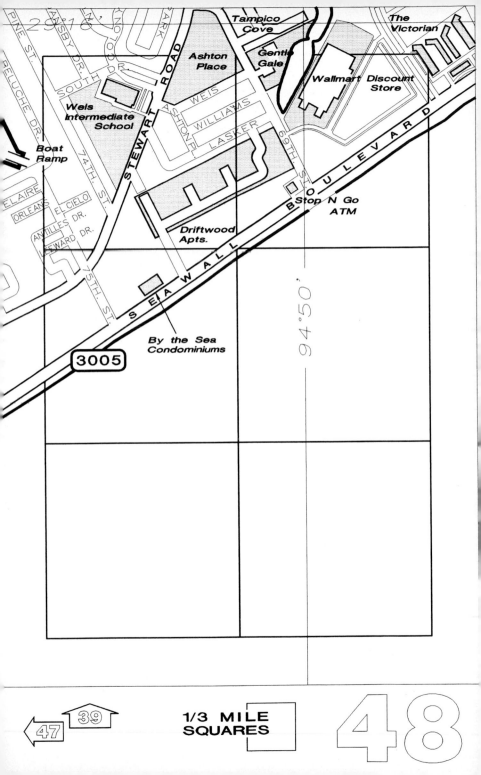

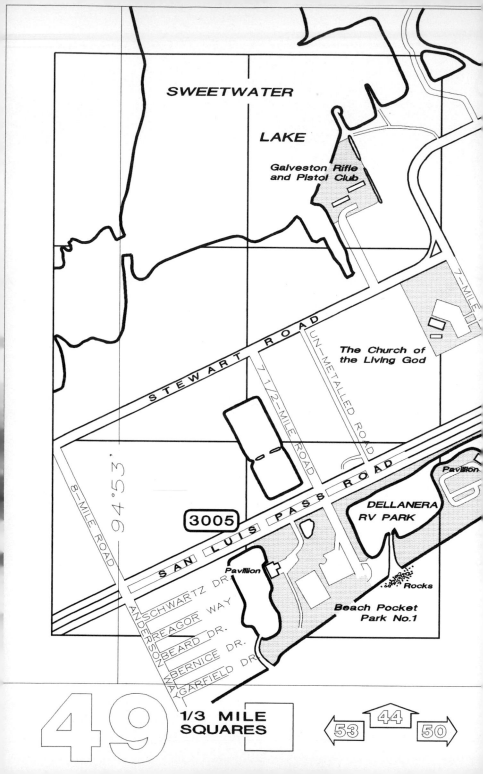

SWEETWATER

LAKE

Galveston Rifle
and Pistol Club

7-MILE

The Church of
the Living God

STEWART ROAD

UN-METALLED ROAD

7 1/2-MILE ROAD

94°53'

8-MILE ROAD

3005

SAN LUIS PASS ROAD

Pavilion

DELLANERA
RV PARK

ANDERSON WAY

SCHWARTZ DR.

REAGOR WAY

BEARD DR.

BERNICE DR.

GARFIELD DR.

Pavilion

Rocks

Beach Pocket
Park No.1

49

1/3 MILE
SQUARES

53   44   50

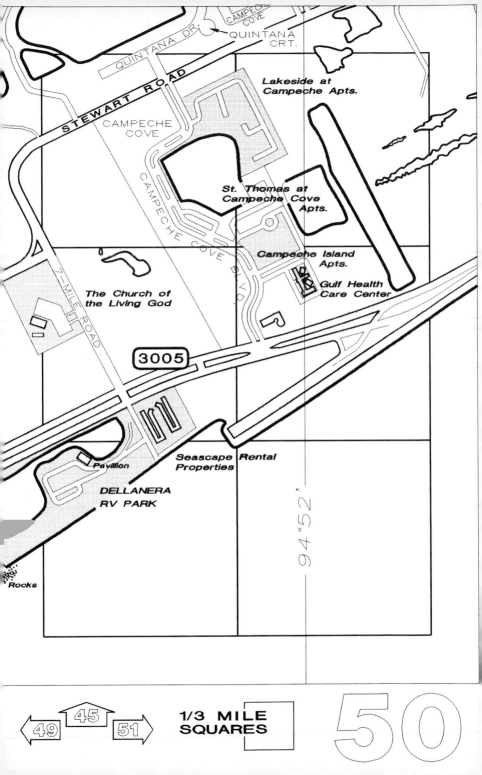

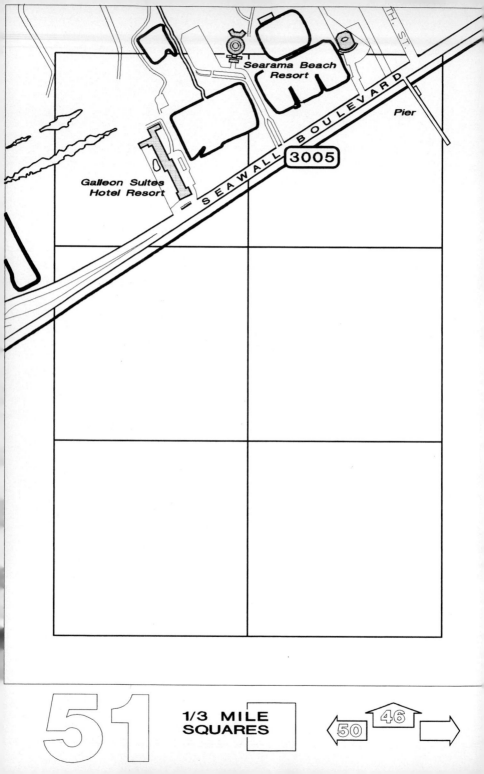

Searama Beach
Resort

Pier

Galleon Suites
Hotel Resort

SEAWALL BOULEVARD

3005

TH. ST.

51

1/3 MILE
SQUARES

50 46

The Ferry 'Robert C. Lanier'
Bolivar Peninsular Free Ferry Service

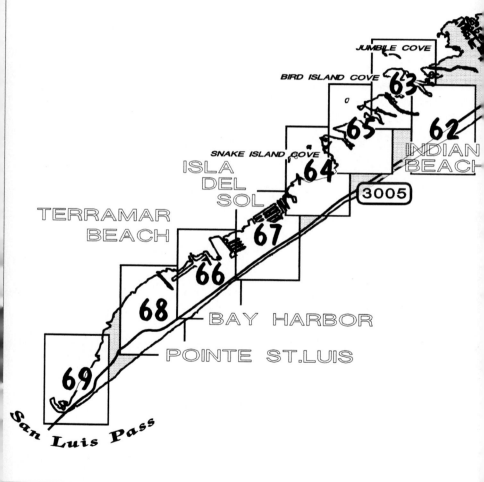

GALVESTON
WEST BAY

JUMBLE COVE

BIRD ISLAND COVE

63

65

SNAKE ISLAND COVE

62

INDIAN
BEACH

ISLA
DEL
SOL

64

3005

TERRAMAR
BEACH

67

66

68

BAY HARBOR

POINTE ST. LUIS

69

San Luis Pass

THE ISLAND:

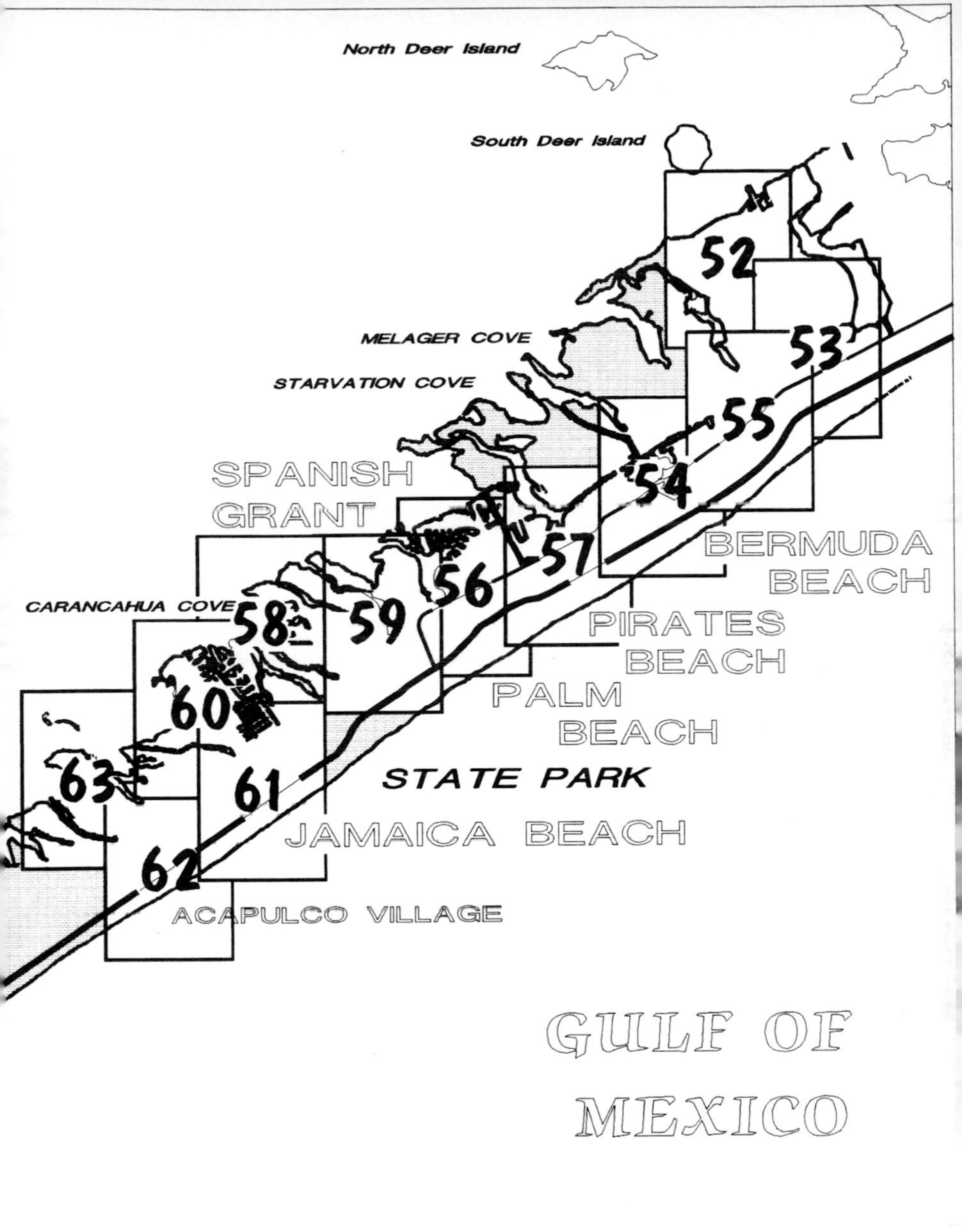

North Deer Island

South Deer Island

52

MELAGER COVE

53

STARVATION COVE

55

54

SPANISH GRANT

57

56

BERMUDA BEACH

CARANCAHUA COVE

58

59

PIRATES BEACH

60

PALM BEACH

63

61

STATE PARK

62

JAMAICA BEACH

ACAPULCO VILLAGE

GULF OF MEXICO

| 0 | 1 | 2 | 3 | 4 | 5 |

MILES

KEY TO MAP PAGES

A

Anderson Way (8 Mile Rd)	53D
Anderson Way R	52B,53A
Augusten Rd	54B

B

Barcelona E.	54C
Beard	53F
Bermuda Beach Dr	54E
Bernice	53F
Binnacle Way	52A
Buena Vista Dr E	54F
Buena Vista Dr W	54F

C

Camina Real	54A
Camina Famosa	54C
Carlotta Ct.	54C
Charlie	55A
Concho	54A
Conquistador	54A

D

Dale St.	55A
David St.	55A
Doz Drive	54A
Dubloon Ave.	54A

E

El Capitan	54A
Elena Court	54C

G

Galleon	54A
Garfield	53F

H

Homrighaus Dr	53A,55A

J

Jane Rd	54F
Jean Drive West	54B,55C
Jenkins Rd	54A
John Reynolds Cir	54F
John Reynolds Rd	54E

M

Madrid E.	54C
Marcia Court	54C

O

Ostermayer Rd	54A,55A

P

Pabst Rd	54C
Pean St.	54F

R

Rachel	54E
Reagor Way	53F

S

San Luis Pass Rd	53E,54D
San Luis Pass Rd	55D
Santiago Circle	54C
Schwartz Drive	53F
Sonny Drive N.	55A
Sonny Drive S.	55B
Spanish Grant Blvd.	54D
Spanish Main Blvd.	54C
Sportman Rd	52A
Stewart Rd	53D,54B
Stewart Rd	55B
Sunny Drive S.	55C

Anderson Ways to SPANISH GRANT & BERMUDA BEACH

T

Toledo E.	54C
Tres Drive	54A

U

Uno Drive	54A

V

Ventura Dr E.	54D
Ventura Dr W	54F
Viking Drive	54B,55E

Z

Zinglemann Rd	55A

8 Mile Rd (Anderson Way)	53D
9 Mile Rd	55A
10 Mile Rd	54B

Street Location

Gary's 8-Mile Road
Boat Camp

SPORTMAN ROAD

ANDERSON WAYS ROAD

Gangs

Bayou

29°15'

94°54'

HOMRIGHAUS ROAD

52 1/2 MILE
SQUARES

54 53

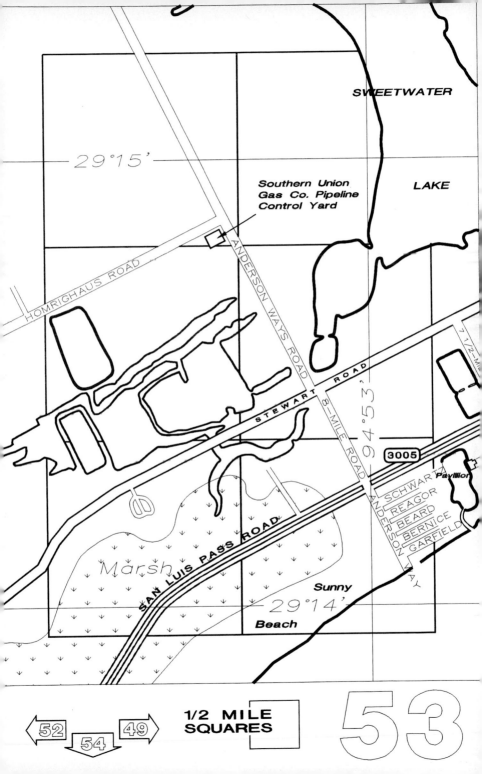

SWEETWATER

29°15'

Southern Union
Gas Co. Pipeline
Control Yard

LAKE

HOMRIGHAUS ROAD

ANDERSON WAYS ROAD

7 1/2 Mile

STEWART ROAD

8-MILE ROAD

29°4'53"

3005

ANDERSON

SCHWAR
REAGOR
BEARD
BERNICE
GARFIELD

Pavilion

WAY

San Luis Pass Road

Marsh

Sunny

29°14'

Beach

52 54 49

1/2 MILE
SQUARES

53

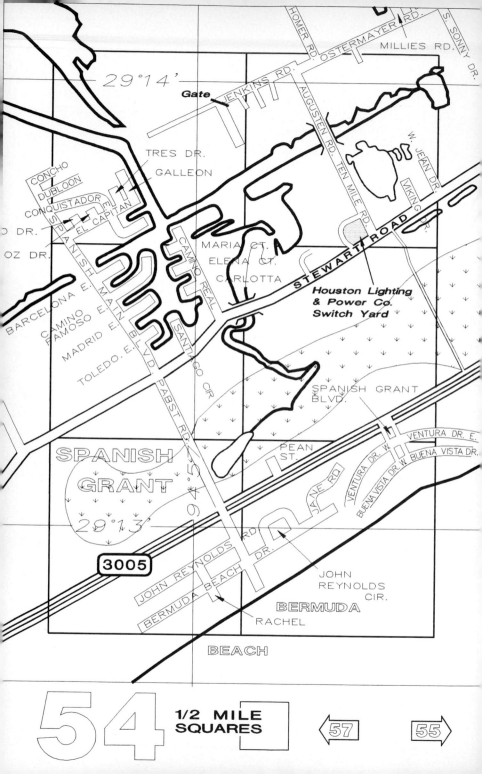

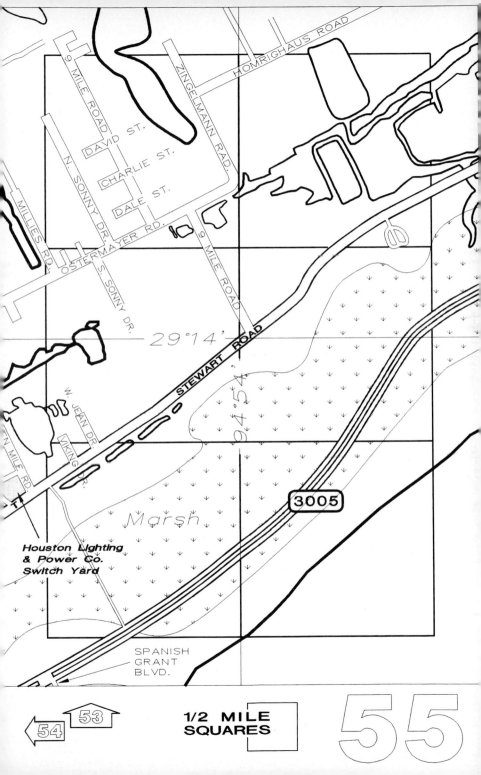

HOMRIGHAUS ROAD

9 MILE ROAD

ZINGELMANN RAD.

DAVID ST.

CHARLIE ST.

DALE ST.

N. SONNY DR.

S. SONNY DR.

OSTERMAYER RD.

MILLIES RD.

9 MILE ROAD

STEWART ROAD

29°14'

94°54'

W. JEAN DR.

VIKING DR.

9 MILE RD.

3005

Marsh

**Houston Lighting
& Power Co.
Switch Yard**

SPANISH
GRANT
BLVD.

53

54

1/2 MILE
SQUARES

55

A

Anchor Way	58E

B

Barbados Way	58E
Barataria	57E
Bayside Way	58E
Bayside Way E.	58E
Bayside Way W.	58E
Binnacle Court	57A
Bucaneer Blvd.	56D,57E

C

Campeche Blvd.	57E
Carthegena Way	56B
Christmas Tree Point Rd	56A
Cove Lane	56B
Crossbones Cir	56A
Cutlass Lane	56B
Cutwater	57A

D

Doubloon Ave.	56B
Duncan Way	56F

E

Eagle Lane	57F
Eckert Drive	57A
El Lago Drive	56E

F

Fiddler Crab Ln	57E
Flamingo Way	58E
Flounder Way	58E
Foremast Drive	57A

G

Ghost Crab Ln	57E
Grambo Blvd.	56B
Grand Terre	57E

J

Jamaica Cove Rd	58E
Jibstay	57A
Jolly Roger Cir	56A
Jolly Roger Rd	58E

K

Krepeer C. C.	56B

L

Lanyard	57A
Las Palmas	56F
Las Palmas Blvd	56E
Long Tom Blvd.	57E
Lucia	56C

M

Mason Rouge	57E
Miramar Drive	56E
Moyene Place	57A
Muscatee Circle	56A
Mutiny Lane	56F,57E

O

Oleander Drive	56F

P

Pelican Lane	56F
Pelican Rd	58E
Petite Circle	56A
Pirates Beach Blvd .	56C,57E
Pirates Beach Ct	56D
Pirates Drive	56F
Pompano Way	58E

R

Raguer Blvd.	57E
Rigaud	56C

PIRATES BEACH, PALM BEACH & THE STATE PARK

S

San Domingo	56F,57E
Sandcrab Ln	57F
Sandpiper Ln	56F
Seabull	56 F
Settgast Rd	57B
Spanish Main Blvd.	58E
Spoonville Lane	56F
Stewart Rd	56C,57B
Stewart Rd	59D
Surf Drive	56F

T

Tampico Way	58E
Termini Rd	56E,57D
Tortuga Way	58E
Treasure Circle	56A

V

Vista Blvd.	56F

W

West Bayside	58E
Windlass Circle	57A
Windlass Court	56A,57A

11 Mile Rd	57A
12 Mile Rd	56B
13 Mile Rd	56E,59D

Street Location

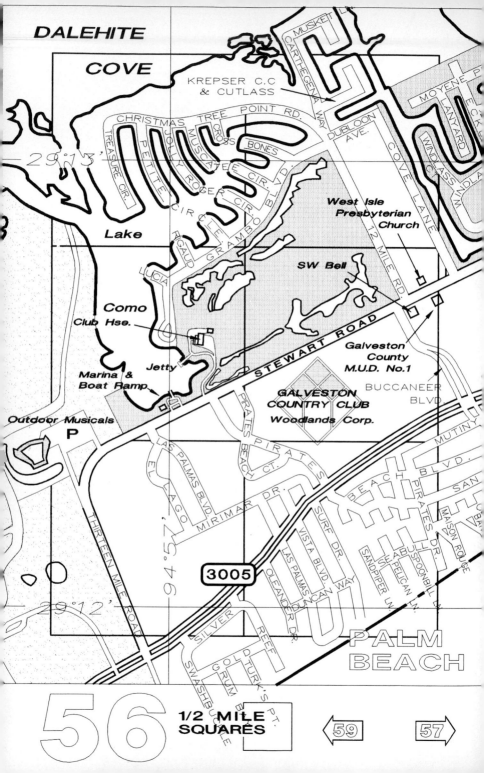

DALEHITE
COVE

KREPSER C.C & CUTLASS

MUSKET LN.
CARTHEGENA WAY

MOYENE PL.
PEKO PL.
LANYARD
WINDLASS
WINDLASS
WINDLASS

CHRISTMAS TREE POINT RD.
JOLLY CROSS
MUSCATEE CIR.
ROGER CIR.
BONES
DUBLOON AVE.
COVE LANE

TREASURE CIR.
PETITE CIRCLE
RIGAUD
GRAMBY BLVD.
LUCIA

Lake

West Isle
Presbyterian
Church

SW Bell

12 MILE RD.

Como
Club Hse.

Jetty

Marina &
Boat Ramp

Outdoor Musicals
P

STEWART ROAD

Galveston
County
M.U.D. No.1

GALVESTON
COUNTRY CLUB
Woodlands Corp.

BUCCANEER
BLVD.

PIRATES BEACH CT.
PIRATES

LAS PALMAS BLVD.
EL LAGO
MIRIMAR DR.
VISTA BLVD.
SURF DR.
LAS PALMAS
DUNCAN WAY
OLEANDER DR.

BEACH
BLVD.
PIRATES DR.
SAN
MAISON ROUGE
MUTINY

SEABULL
SANDPIPER LN.
PELICAN
SPOONBILL
MAISON ROUGE

THIRTEEN MILE ROAD

94°57'

3005

29°12'

SILVER
REEF
GOLD
GRUM
TURK'S PT.
SWASHBUCKLE

PALM
BEACH

56
1/2 MILE SQUARES

◁ 59

57 ▷

29°13'

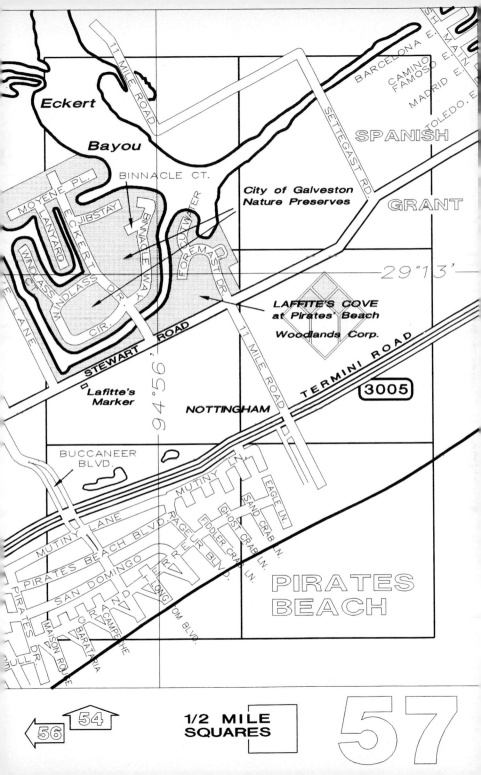

Eckert

Bayou

11 MILE ROAD

BARCELONA E.
CAMINO FAMOSO
MADRID E.
TOLEDO E.
MAIN
SPANISH
GRANT

SETTEGAST RD.

BINNACLE CT.

City of Galveston
Nature Preserves

MOYENE PL.
LANYARD
ECKERT DR.
JIBSTAY
BINNACLE WAY
BINNACLE DR.
FORE TOPWATER
FOREMAST DR.
WINDLASS CT.
WINDLASS CIR.
YM LANE

29°13'

LAFFITE'S COVE
at Pirates' Beach

Woodlands Corp.

STEWART ROAD

94°56'

Lafitte's
Marker

NOTTINGHAM

11 MILE ROAD

TERMINI ROAD

3005

BUCCANEER
BLVD.

MUTINY LN.
EAGLE LN.
SAND CRAB LN.
GHOST CRAB LN.
FIDDLER CRAB LN.
RAGUR BLVD.

MUTINY LANE

PIRATES BEACH BLVD.

SAN DOMINGO

TERRE

LONG TOM BLVD.

A CAMPECHE

BARATARIA

MAISON ROUGE

PIRATES DR.

BULL

PIRATES
BEACH

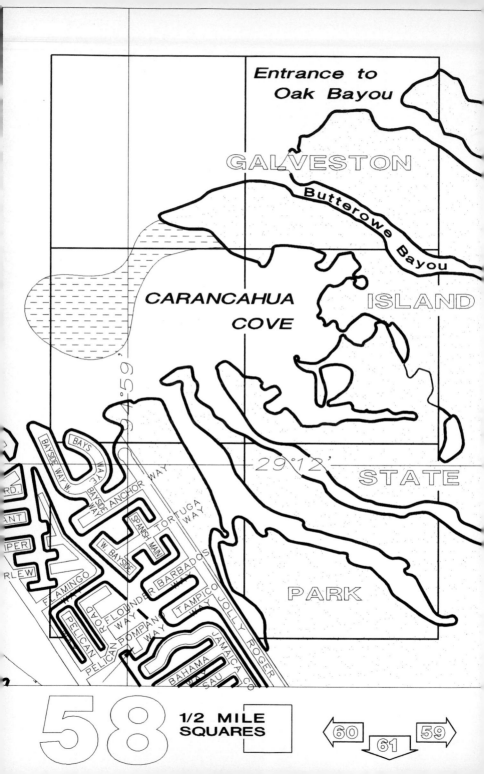

Entrance to
Oak Bayou

GALVESTON

Butterowe Bayou

ISLAND

CARANCAHUA
COVE

94°59'

29°12'

STATE

BAYS WAY E.
BAYS WAY
BAYSIDE WAY W.
BAYSIDE ANCHOR WAY
SPANSH MAN
TORTUGA WAY
W. BAYSIDE
BARBADOS WAY
FLOUNDER WAY
FLAMINGO
PELICAN ROAD
POMPANO WAY
PELICAN
TAMPICO WAY
JOLLY ROGER
JAMAICA CO
BAHAMA WAY
NASSAU
RD.
ANT
PER
RLEW

PARK

58 1/2 MILE
    SQUARES

60 61 59

A

Albatros Rd	60B
Anchor Way	60B
Antigua Avenue	62D

B

Bahama Way	60D,61A
Barbados Way	60D
Bayside Way	60B
Bayside Way E.	60B
Bayside Way W.	60B
Blackbeard Rd	61D
Bob Smith Rd	60A,61A
Bristow Blvd	61E
Bucaneer	61B
Bucaneer Drive	62D
Burmuda Way	61A

C

Cabeza De Vaca	60D,61A
Captain Bligh Rd	61D
Captain Hook	62C
Captain Hook Rd	61D
Captain Kidd	62B
Captain Kidd Rd	61B
Cormorant Rd	60A
Curlew Rd	60B

D

Davy Jones Rd	61A
De Vaca Lane E.	62C
De Vaca Lane W.	62E
Dolphin	62D

E

Edward Teach Rd	61D

F

Flamingo Way	60D
Fletcher Chrstian Rd	61D
Flounder Way	60D
Frances Drake Rd	61B

G

Giel Giel	61E,62D
Gulf Blvd.	62D

H

Habia Drive	61E,62D
Henry Morgan Rd	61B

I

Indian Beach Ct	63F
Indian Beach Dr	63F

J

Jamaica Beach Rd	61D
Jamaica Cove Rd	60D,61B
Jamaica Inn	61A
Jean Lafitte	62D
Jean Lafitte Rd	61B
John Davis Rd	61B
John Silver Rd	61B
Jolly Roger Rd	61A

K

Kingston Way	60D,61A
Kiva Rd	62C

L

Lewis Scot Rd	61B

M

Managua Way	60D,61A
Manevelt Rd	61B
Marina Rd	60A
Mariner	62D
Mermaid	62D
Mitote Drive	62C,63F
Moby Dick Rd	61A
Montego Way	60D,61A

JAMAICA BEACH, INDIAN BEACH & ACAPULCO VILLAGE

N

Nassau Way	61A
Nautilus	62B

O

Ocean View	62D

P

Pelican Rd	60D
Pelican Way	60D
Pompano Way	60D
Ponce De Leon Rd	61A
Porpoise Blvd.	62D

R

Redfish Drive	60D
Roger Rd	60B

S

San Luis Pass Rd	62C
Sandpiper	60B
Sandpiper Rd	62D
Seagull	62 D
Shaman Rd	62B
Spanish Main Blvd.	60B

T

Tahiti Way	60D,61A
Tampico	62D
Tampico Way	60D
Tern Rd	60A
Tortuga Way	60B
Trinidad Way	61A

V

Vera Cruz	62D

W

Warrior Court	62B
Warrior Drive	62B
West Bayside	60B
West Beach Rd	61D

16 Mile Rd	61E
3005	61C

Street Location

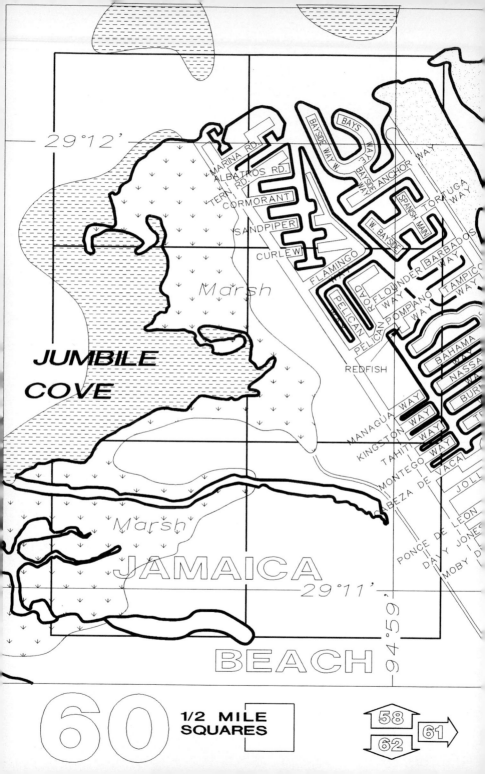

29°12'

MARINA RD.
ALBATROS RD.
TERN RD.
CORMORANT
SANDPIPER
CURLEW

BAYSIDE WAY W.
BAYS
ANCHOR WAY
BAYSIDE WAY E.
W. BAYSIDE
SPANISH MAN
TORTUGA WAY

FLAMINGO WAY
FLOUNDER WAY
BARBADOS WAY
PELICAN RD.
POMPANO WAY
TAMPICO WAY
PELICAN WAY

Marsh

JUMBILE

COVE

REDFISH

BAHAMA WAY
NASSAU
BURM
MANAGUA WAY
KINGSTON WAY
TAHITI WAY
MONTEGO WAY
CABEZA DE VACA
JOLL
PONCE DE LEON
DAVY JONES
MOBY D

Marsh

JAMAICA
29°11'

94°59'

BEACH

60

1/2 MILE SQUARES

58
62
61

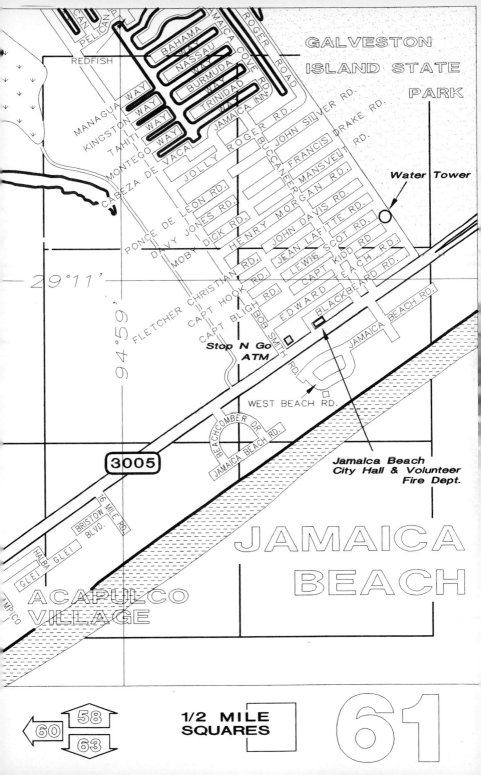

GALVESTON ISLAND STATE PARK

JAMAICA BEACH

ACAPULCO VILLAGE

Water Tower

Stop N Go
ATM

Jamaica Beach
City Hall & Volunteer
Fire Dept.

WEST BEACH RD.

3005

REDFISH

PELICAN
AMERICAN
BAHAMA WAY
NASSAU WAY
BURMUDA WAY
TRINIDAD WAY
JAMAICA COVE RD.
ROGER ROAD
JAMAICA INN
JAMAICA WAY

MANAGUA WAY
KINGSTON WAY
TAHITI WAY
MONTEGO WAY
CABEZA DE VACA
PONCE DE LEON RD.
DAVY JONES RD.
MOBY DICK RD.
FLETCHER CHRISTIAN RD.
CAPT HOOK RD.
CAPT BLIGH RD.
BOB SMITH RD.

JOLLY ROGER RD.
BUCCANEER RD.
JOHN SILVER RD.
FRANCIS DRAKE RD.
MANSVELT RD.
HENRY MORGAN RD.
JOHN DAVIS RD.
JEAN LAFITTE RD.
LEWIS SCOT RD.
CAPT. KIDD RD.
TEACH RD.
BLACKBEARD RD.
EDWARD
JAMAICA BEACH RD.

BEACHCOMBER DR.
JAMAICA BEACH RD.

16 MILE RD.
BRISTOW BLVD.
GLEI
HALBA GLEI
TAMPICO

29°11'
94°59'

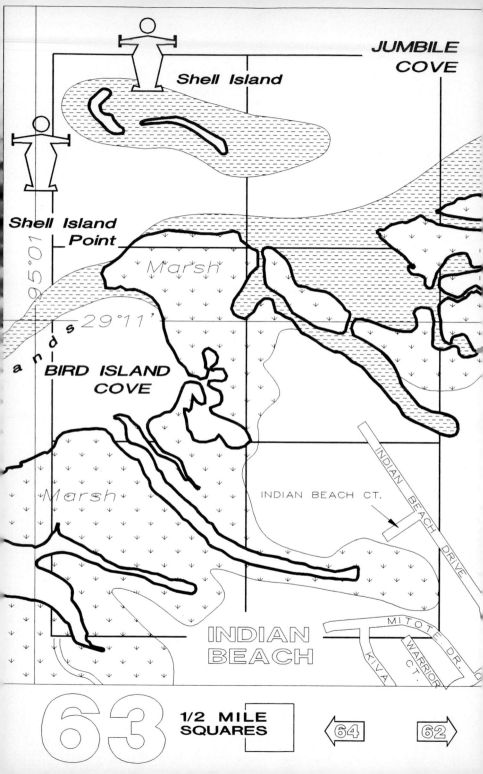

JUMBILE
COVE

Shell Island

Shell Island
Point

95°01'

Marsh

29°11'

a n d s

BIRD ISLAND
COVE

Marsh

INDIAN BEACH CT.

INDIAN BEACH DRIVE

MITOTE DR.

WARRIOR CT.

KIVA

INDIAN
BEACH

63

1/2 MILE
SQUARES

64

62

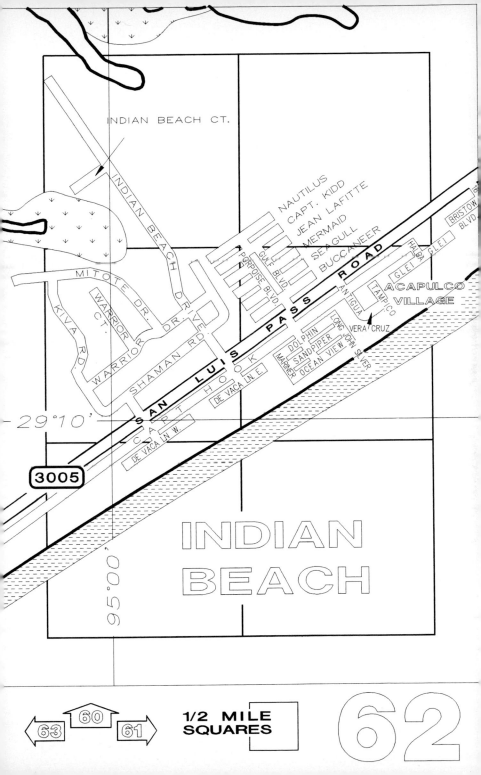

INDIAN BEACH CT.

INDIAN BEACH DRIVE

MITOTE DR.

WARRIOR CT.

KIVA RD.

WARRIOR DR.

SHAMAN RD.

SAN LUIS PASS ROAD

CART HOOK

DE VACA LN. E.

DE VACA LN W.

29°10'

3005

95°00'

NAUTILUS
CAPT. KIDD
JEAN LAFITTE
MERMAID
SEA GULL
BUCCANEER

PORPOISE BLVD.

GULF BLVD.

BRISTOW BLVD.

HALDA

GLEI GLEI

GLEI

ANTIGUA

TAMPICO

ACAPULCO VILLAGE

VERA CRUZ

DOLPHIN
SANDPIPER
LONG JOHN SILVER
MARINER
OCEAN VIEW

INDIAN BEACH

A

Amino St.	66D
Antasoosa Key	67A

B

Bay Point Dr.	67C
Bay Vista Dr.	67C
Brewster Key Rd.	67A
Bridge Harbor Dr.	67C
Bueno St.	66D,67E
Burnst Dr.	67B

C

Camino St.	67E
Catalina Dr.	68E
Chiquita St.	66B
Comanche Dr.	67C
Concho Key	64E,67E
Coronado Ct.	68D
Courageous Ln.	68E
Cuadro St.	67E

D

Dawson Dr.	67C
Deaf Place	67A
Defender Ln.	68E

E

Ector Dr.	67D

F

Fort Bend Dr.	67A
Fresca St.	66D,67E
Frio Dr.	67A

G

Galcean	66C
Grayson Dr.	67D
Guadalupe Dr.	67A

H

Hardin Dr.	67D

I

Ilsa Del Sol Dr.	67 C
Ilsa View	67C
Intrepid Lane	68E
Island Court Dr	67C

J

Jackson Dr.	67D

K

Kennedy Dr.	67D
Kent Dr.	67D

L

Laguna Dr.	67C
Lampasas Dr.	67D
Liberty Dr.	67D
Lunes St.	66B

M

Martes St.	66B
Mason Dr.	67B
Matagorda Dr.	67B
Mendocino Dr	68C
Miramar St.	67E
Monterey Court	68D

N

Navarro Dr.	67B
Nueces Dr.	67C

O

Obra Dr.	67E

TERRAMAR BEACH, BAY HARBOR, SEA ISLE, ISLA DEL SOL, & POINTE ST. LUIS

Street Location

Maggies Point

MAGGIES
COVE

Marsh

Snake Island

SNAKE ISLAND
COVE

Marsh

95°02'

29°09'

3005

CONCHO KEY

KEY DR.

NET PA

REEV

SAN J

64 1/2 MILE
SQUARES

63
65

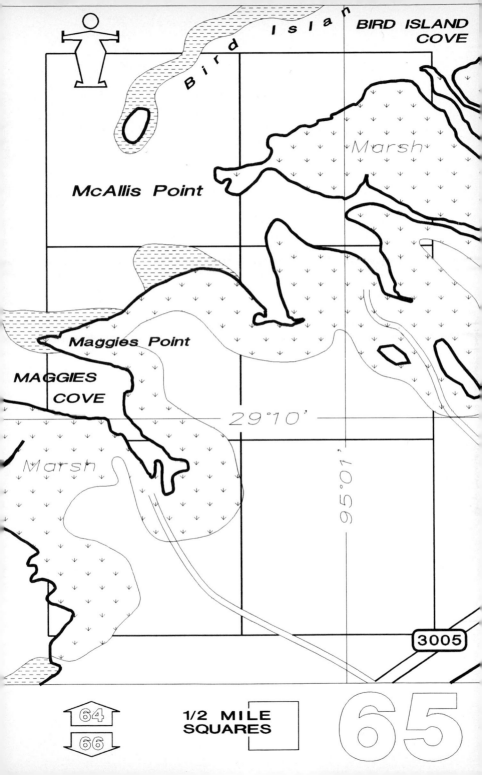

Bird Island

BIRD ISLAND
COVE

Marsh

McAllis Point

Maggies Point

MAGGIES
COVE

29°10'

95°01'

Marsh

3005

64
66

1/2 MILE
SQUARES

65

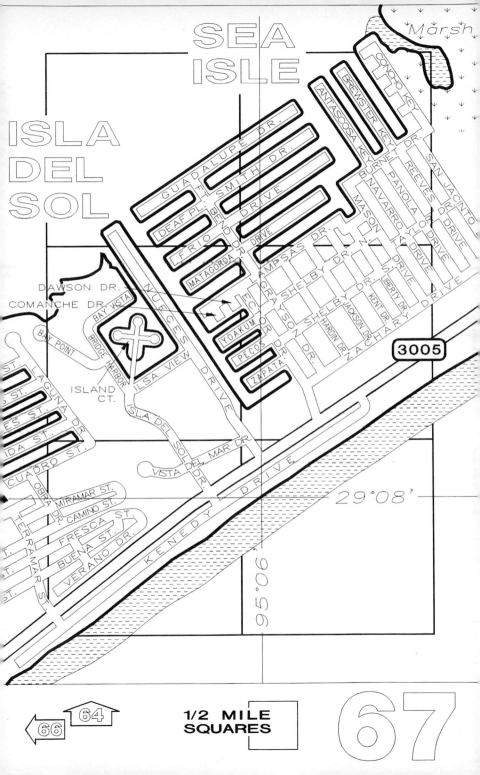

SEA ISLE

ISLA DEL SOL

Marsh

CONCHO KEY

BREWSTER KEY

ANTASCOSA KEY

BURNET DR.

REEVES DR. DRIVE

SAN JACINTO

GUADALUPE DR.

DEAF PL.

SMITH DR.

FRIO DRIVE

MATAGORDA DR.

NAVARRO DRIVE

PANOLA DRIVE

MASON DR.

DRIVE

DRIVE

LAMPSAS DR.

GRAYSON DR.

SHELBY DR.

N.

LIBERTY DR.

KENT DR.

GRAYSON DR.

HARDIN DR.

JACKSON DR.

DAWSON DR.

COMANCHE DR.

BAY VISTA

NUECES

YOAKUM DR.

PECOS DR.

ZAPATA

SHELBY DR.

HARDIN DR.

3005

BAY POINT

BRIDGE HARBOR

ISLA VIEW DRIVE

ISLAND CT.

LA LAGUNA DR.

ST.

ES ST.

DA ST.

CUADRO ST.

OBRA

ISLA DEL SOL DR.

VISTA DEL MAR DR.

VISTA DR.

MIRAMAR ST.

CAMINO ST.

FRESCA ST.

BUENA ST.

VERANO DR.

KENEDY DRIVE

29°08'

95°06'

TERRAMAR ST.

ST.

1/2 MILE SQUARES

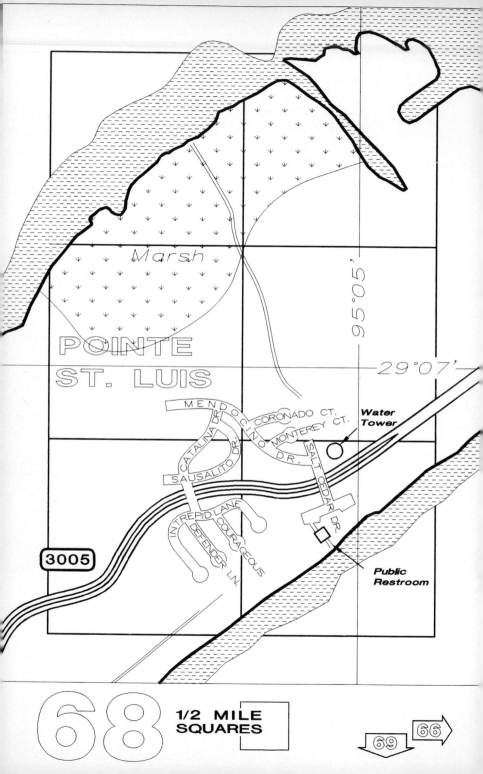

Marsh

POINTE
ST. LUIS

MENDOCINO DR.
CORONADO CT.
CATALINA DR.
MONTEREY CT.
SAUSALITO DR.
SALT CEDAR DR.

**Water
Tower**

INTREPID LANE
DEFENDER LN.
COURAGEOUS

95°05'

29°07'

**Public
Restroom**

3005

68 1/2 MILE
SQUARES

69 66

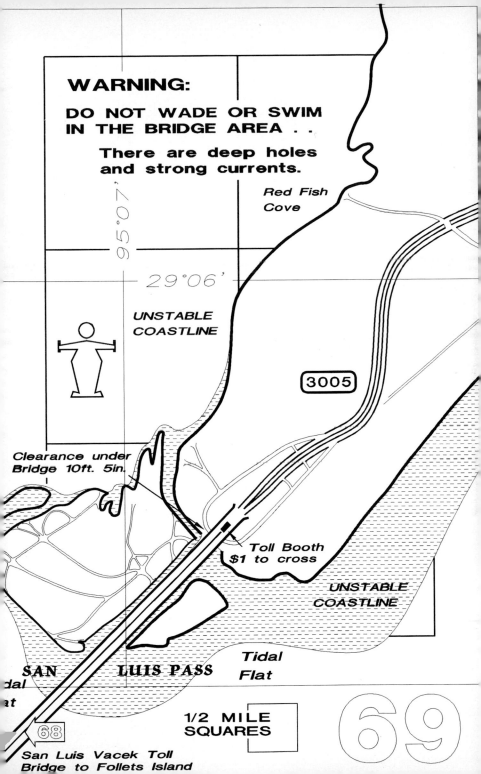

WARNING:

DO NOT WADE OR SWIM IN THE BRIDGE AREA . .

There are deep holes and strong currents.

Red Fish Cove

95°07'

29°06'

UNSTABLE COASTLINE

3005

Clearance under Bridge 10ft. 5in.

Toll Booth
$1 to cross

UNSTABLE COASTLINE

SAN   **LUIS PASS**

Tidal Flat

dal
at

68

1/2 MILE
SQUARES

69

San Luis Vacek Toll Bridge to Follets Island

A

Street	Page
Adler Circle	40
Admiral Circle	TB
Airport Blvd.	37,38
Albacore Ave	12,20
Albatros Rd	60
Alice St.	47
Amino St.	66
Antasoosa Key	67
Anchor Way	58,60
Anderson Way	49
Anderson Way R	52,53
Antigua Avenue	62
Antilles Drive	47,48
Apfel Park Rd	13
Ashton Place	48
Augusten Rd	54
Austin Avenue	29
Avalon Way	2
Avenue A	10-12,20
(Water St.)	21AB
Avenue B	12E
Avenue C 1	1,12,20
(Mechanic St.)	21,22A
Avenue D	11,12,20
(Market St.)	21,22
Avenue E	12,18,20
(Post Office St.)	21-23
Avenue F	12,18-20
(Church St.)	21-23
Avenue G	18-23
(Winnie St.)	29
Avenue H	19-21
(Ball St.)	22,23,29
Avenue I	19-21
(Sealy St.)	22,23,29
Avenue J	22,23
Avenue K	20-23
	28-30
Avenue L	20-22
	28-31
Avenue M	20-22
	29-31
Avenue M1/2	21-22
	29-31
Avenue N	21,22
(Ursuline St.)	30-32
Avenue N1/2	21,22
	29-31,38
Avenue O	22,29-32
	38
Avenue O1/2	29-33,38
Avenue P	29-33,38
(Benardo De Galvez Ave.)	
Avenue P1/2	29-32
Avenue Q	29-32,39
Avenue Q1/2	29-32
	38-40
Avenue R	29-32
	39,40
Avenue R1/2	30-32,40
Avenue S	30-1,40-1
Avenue S1/2	30-1,40-1
Avenue T	31,41,40
Avenue T1/2	41,40
Avenue U	40,41
Azalea Court	39

B

Street	Page
Backbay Circle	38
Backbay Drive	38
Bahama Way	60,61
Ball St.	19-23
(Ave. H)	28,29
Barbados Way	58,60
Barcelona E.	54
Bamar Lane	24
Bamaku Bend	TB
Bamboo	TA,TB
Barataria	57
Barracuda Ave.	12
Baudeliare Cir.	47
Bay Meadows	35,44
Bay Point Drive	67
Bay Vista Drive	67
Bayou/Front Ln	38
Bayou Circle Dr	28
Bayou Homes Dr	39
Bayou Shore Dr	28
Bayside Ave.	25,26
Bayside Way	58,60
Bayside Way E.	58,60
Bayside Way W.	58,60
Beacon	46
Beard Drive	49
Beard	53
Beech	37
Belo	29
Beluche Drive	38,47,48
Bermuda Beach Dr	54
Bernardo De Galvez Ave.	29,30
(Ave. P)	31-33,38
Bernice	53
Bernice Drive	49
Bertolino's View	22
(10th. St.)	
Binnacle Court	57
Binnacle Way	52
Biovu Drive	39
Blackbeard Rd	61
Bluebonnet Ct	39
Blume St.	25,46,51
(89th)	
Bob Smith Rd	60,61
Boddeker Drive	4,5
(South Jetty Rd)	
Bonanza	46
Bonita Ave.	12
Bora Bora	TB
Borden Ave.	28,29
Bowie Drive	29
Brandner St.	9
Brewster Key Rd	67
Bridge Harbor Dr	67
Bristow Blvd	61
Broadway St.	19-21,29
Broome Rd	44,45
Bryan	35
Bucaneer	61
Bucaneer Blvd.	56,57
Bucaneer Drive	62
Buena Vista Dr E	54
Buena Vista Dr W	54
Bueno St.	66,67
Burmuda Way	61
Burnst Drive	67

C

Street	Page
Cabeza De Vaca	60,61
Cadena Drive	45
Caduceus Place	41
Camina Real	54
Camina Famosa	54
Camino St.	67
Campbell Lane	28
Campeche Blvd.	57
Campeche Cir	45
Campeche Cove	45
Campeche Cove Blvd	50
Campeche Dr	45
Campeche Est	45
Captain Bligh Rd	61
Captain Hook	62
Captain Hook Rd	61
Captain Kidd	62
Captain Kidd Rd	61
Carlotta Ct.	54
Carthegena Way	56
Castaway	TA
Catalina Drive	68
Catamaran	TA
Cedar Lawn Dr S	30
Cedar Lawn Cir	29,30
Cedar LawnDrN	30
Central City Blvd.	39
Channelview Dr	25,26
Chantilly Circle	47
Charlie	55
Chataignon Pl	22
(13th. St.)	
Cherokee	37,38
Chiquita St.	66
Christmas Tree Point Rd	56
Christopher Columbus	11,22
Church St.	12,18,19
(Ave. F)	20-23
Cloud Lane	44,45
Coconut	TA
Colony Park Cir	39
Colony Park Dr	39
Comanche Dr	67
Commander	TA
Concho Key	64,67
Concho	54
Conquistador	54
Copilot Lane	35
Copra	TA
Coral Way	TB
Cormorant Rd	60
Coronado Court	68
Cosy Cove	24
Courageous Ln	68
Cove Lane	56
Crockett Blvd.	40,41
Crossbones Cir	56
Cuadro St.	67
Curlew Rd	60
Cutlass Lane	56
Cutwater	57
Cypress Drive	39

D

Street	Page
Dale St.	55
Dansby Drive	39
Darcy Drive	35
Darrell Royal Blvd.	11,12
Davy Jones Rd	61
David St.	55
Dawson Drive	67
De Vaca Lane E.	62
De Vaca Lane W.	62
Deaf Place	67
Defender Lane	68
Diamond Drive	TA
Diamond Head Dr	
Dolphin	62
Dolphin Ave.	12
Dominique Dr	46,47
Doubloon Ave.	56
Doz Drive	54
Driftwood Lane	39
Dubloon Ave.	54
Duncan Way	56

E

Street	Page
East Beach Dr	4,12-14
Easterly Drive	TA
Eagle Lane	57
Eckert Drive	57
Ector Drive	67
Edward Teach Rd	61

CONSOLIDATED STREET LIST

.... continued

Palm Circle	40	Schaper St.	45	Trinidad Way	61		
Palmetto	TA	Schwartz Drive	53	Trout Ave.	12		
Panola Drive	67	Seabull	56	Tuna Ave.	12		
Papeete	TB	Seagull	62	Turn Drive	40		
Paradise Drive	TB	Sealy St.	19-,21				
Park St.	39	*(Ave. I)*	22,23,29				
Park Lane	39	Seawall E. Blvd.	3,12,13				
Pean St.	54	Seawall Blvd.	22-3,32-3	**U**			
Pearl Lane	2		40-42,47				
Pelican Island Causeway	7,18		48,50,51	University Blvd.	12,23		
Pelican Lane	56	Seawolf Pkw	1,8,9	Uno Drive	54		
Pelican Rd	58,60	Settgast Rd	57	Ursuline St.	21,22,30		
Pelican Way	60	Shaman Rd	62	*(Ave. N)*	31,32		
Penzoil Rd	10	Shelby Dr South	67				
Petite Circle	56	Shelby Dr North	67				
Pine St.	38,48	Sherman Blvd.	41				
(74th St.)		Short Reach	TB				
Pilot Lane	35	Sias Drive	41	**V**			
Piper	37	Sidney St.	39				
Pirates Beach Blvd .	56,57	Skipper St.	35	Valer Drive	66		
Pirates Beach Ct	56	Sky Lane	35	Ventura Dr E.	54		
Pirates Drive	56	Skymaster Rd	38	Ventura Dr W	54		
Pompano Ave.	12	Smith Drive	67	Vera Cruz	62		
Pompano Way	58,60	Sonny Drive N.	55	Verano Drive	67		
Ponce De Leon Rd	61	Sonny Drive S.	55	Victory Ave.	39		
Poplar Drive	38,39	South Drive	48	Vida St.	66,67		
Porpoise Blvd.	62	South Shore Dr	28	Viking Drive	54,55		
Port Trinidad	66	South Jetty Rd	4,5	Vista Blvd.	56		
Port O'Call	TAE	*(Boddeker Drive)*		Vista Del Mar Dr	67		
Post Office St.	12,18,21	Spanish Grant Blvd.	54				
(Ave. E)		Spanish Main Blvd.	54,58,60				
Princeton St.	47	Spanish Wells	66				
Preston	35	Spoonville Lane	56				
Pruitt Drive	25,26	Sportman Rd	52	**W**			
		St. Mary's Blvd.	11,22				
		(8th St.)		Wahini	TB		
		Stewart Rd	29,39,40	Walsh Lane	26		
Q			45-50,53	Warrior Court	62		
			54-58	Warrior Drive	62		
Quayside	TB	Strand St.	11,21	Water St.	10,11,12		
Que Sade St.	66	Suhler Rd	9	*(Ave. A)*	20,21		
Quintana Court	45	Sunny Drive S.	55	Weber Ave.	40		
Quintana Drive	45,50	Surf Drive	56	Weis Drive	48		
		Swan Drive	40	West Bayside	58,60		
		Sycamore Drive	38,39	West Beach Rd	61		
		Sydnor Lane	45	West Dansby Dr	48		
R				Westwood	40		
				Wharton Ave.	29		
Rachel	54	**T**		Whiting Ave.	12		
Raguer Blvd.	57			Williams Drive	48		
Randall	29	Tahiti	TB	Williamsburg Dr	39		
Redfish Drive	60	Tamana	TB	Willow Lane	39		
Reagor Way	49,53	Tahiti Way	60,61	Wilnox St.	27		
Reeves Drive	67	Taylor St.	67	Wimcrest St.	39		
Rice St.	47	Tampico	62	Windlass Circle	57		
Rigaud	56	Tampico Way	58,60	Windlass Court	56,57		
Rojer Rd	60	Tarpon Ave.	12	Windward Way	TB		
Rosenberg Ave.	21	Teal Drive	40	Winnie St.	18-21		
Rosewood Dr	40	Teichman Rd	24,25	*(Ave. G)*	22,23,29		
		Temprano Drive	66	Woodrow Ave.	41		
		Terminal Drive	37,46				
		Termini Rd	56,57				
S		Tern Rd	60				
		Texas Ave.	11,12				
Sabrina St.	66	Tidewater	66	**Y**			
Salt Cedar Dr	68	Tiki Circle	TC				
San Domingo	56,57	Tiki Drive	TA-TC	Yale St.	47		
San Fernando Dr	12	Todd St.	90,10	Yoakum Drive	67		
San Jacinto Dr	12,67	Toledo E.	54	Yucca Drive	38,39		
San Luis Pass Rd	49,62	Tortuga Way	58,60	Yupon	39		
	53-55	Tradewinds Dr	66				
San Marino Dr	12	Tradewinds	45				
San Salito Dr	68	Travel Air Rd	35,36,45				
Sandcrab Ln	57	(99th St.)		**Z**			
Sandpiper	60	Travis Drive	29				
Sandpiper Ln	56	Treasure Circle	56	Zachary Drive	67		
Sandpiper Rd	62	Tremont St.	21,32	Zapata Drive	67		
Santiago Circle	54	(23rd St.)		Zinglemann Rd	55		
		Tres Drive	54				

CONSOLIDATED STREET LIST

NUMBERED STREETS

Street	Ref
1st St.	12,66
2nd St.	12,23,66
3005	61,64-69
3rd St.	12,23
4th Ave.	66,66
4th St.	12,23,66
(Holiday Drive)	
5th St.	11,12
	23,66
6th St.	23,66
(University Blvd.)	
7 Mile Rd	49,50
7th St.	22,23,66
7 1/2 Mile Rd	49
8 Mile Rd	49,53
(Anderson Ways)	
8th St.	11,22
9 Mile Rd	55
9th St.	11,22
10 Mile Rd	54
10th St.	11,22
(Bertolino's View)	
11 Mile Rd	57
11th St.	11,22
12 Mile Rd	56
12th St.	11,22
13 Mile Rd	56,59
13th St.	11,22
14th St.	22
15th St.	22
16th St.	21,22

Street	Ref
16 Mile Rd	61
17th St.	21,22,33
18th St.	21,22,33
19th St.	21,33
20th St.	21,32
21st St.	21,32
22nd St.	21,32
23rd St.	21,32
24th St.	21,32
25th St.	21,32
26th St.	20,21,32
27th St.	20,21,32
28th St.	20,28,32
29th St.	20,31,32
30th St.	20,31,32
31st St.	20,31
32nd St.	20,31
33rd St.	20,31
34th St.	20,31
35th St.	20,31
36th St.	19,20,31
37th St.	19,31
38th St.	19,30,31
39th St.	19,30
(Mike Gaido Blvd.)	
40th St.	31,42
41st St.	19,30,31
42nd St.	19,30,41
43rd St.	19,30,41
44th St.	19,30
45th St.	19,30,41
46th St.	18,30,41
47th St.	29,30,41
48th St.	29,30,41
49th St.	29,30,41
50th St.	29,30,41

Street	Ref
51st St.	18,29,40
52nd St.	29,40
53rd St.	18,29,40
(Mary Moody Northen)	
54th St.	18,29,40
55th St.	29,40
56th St.	29,40
57th St.	28,29,40
59th St.	28,39,40
(Leonard Ave.)	
61st St.	28,39,40
62nd St.	28
63rd St.	28
64th St.	27,28
65th St.	39
67th St.	39
68th St.	38,39
69th St.	38,48
71st St.	27,38
72nd St.	38
73rd St.	38
74th St.	38,48
(Pine St.)	
75th St.	48
77th St.	26,47
79th St.	47
80th St.	47
81st St.	47
83rd St.	37,47
85th St.	25,47
87th St.	46,47
89th St.	25,46,51
91st St.	25
93rd St.	24
99th St.	45
103rd St.	35,44,45

.... continued

Can We Talk?
Good! Let's Get Technical

COLOR IMAGING CENTER

Macintosh:

UMax Super Mac S900 (3); all with 96 MB of ram and state-of-the-art color monitors.

Files accepted on Syquest 44, 88, or 200 MB, Bernoulli, Zip, Jaz, EZ 135, 650 MB optical and compact disks.

Scanning:

Optronics Color-Getter II Pro high resolution drum scanner
Agfa Arcus flatbed scanner

Software:

Macromedia Freehand 7.0
Adobe Photoshop 4.0
Adobe Pagemaker 6.5
Adobe Illustrator 6.0
QuarkXPress 3.3
Corel Draw 7.0

Output:

600 dpi New Gen Turbo laser printer
3M Rainbow color proof printer
Lasermaster Displaymaker - 35" x 108" max.
Imagesetter for film output - 20" x 28"

Telecommunications:

Internet home page and FTP site - www.asapcom.com
Bulletin board - Macintosh IIci
Teleport Mercury modem
Telefinder software, 24hrs/day

Archiving:

Macintosh Performa 630CD
Datadisk CDR-4X CD recorder

FINE PRINTING

Press Department:

Heidelberg 6-Color Speedmaster with coater
4-Color Speedmaster
SORMZ 2-Color
Alcolor Consoles and Gretag Densitometers
All presses 20½" x 29"

Camera Department:

VGC 820 auto vertical camera
Film size - 16" x 20"
24" Dupont film processor

Stripping:

Douthitt Contact Frame
Gretag densitometer (transparent)

Proofing:

3M Matchprint Processor
3M Matchprint Laminator
Theimer OmniVac vacuum frame

Plating:

Kodak negative plate processor
DS Screen - step & repeat machine
Douthitt vacuum frames (2)

Bindery:

Cutters (2), Stahl Folders (2), Omni Binder, Heidelberg Letterpress, 3-hole drill, round corner machine, and shrink wrapper

QUICK PRINT:

- One and two-color Ryobis - 11" x 17"
- Kodak ColorEdge 1550+ copier-printer with EFI Fiery 200i color server. Color laser output
- Kodak 1580 spot color copier-printer
- GBC binding
- Laminating & mounting

ASAP Communications

851 Dairy Ashford   281/497-4661 (phone)
Houston, Texas 77079   281/497-3276 (fax)
asap@asapcom.com (e-mail)